Advanced Mortgage Loan Officer Business Development Practices

Second Edition

Kenneth W. Poole

ISBN 978-0615740317

Published by Charter Publications
www.CharterPublications.com

CONTENTS

About the Author
Kenneth W. Poole

Ken Poole isn't a theorist standing on the sidelines; he's a lifelong mortgage banker who has lived in the trenches of mortgage lending and achieved extraordinary results. This book is straight talk from someone who has learned from his successes and from his mistakes and those of his colleagues during a long mortgage banking career.

During a career that has spanned more than forty years, Ken Poole has become one of the mortgage profession's most credible resources. He has exceptional front line mortgage lending experience as a loan officer, branch manager, area manager and regional manager in both retail and wholesale mortgage

Ken Poole

lending, where he directly supervised and trained mortgage loan officers. He has also managed the due diligence and integration of mortgage operations in the merger of major financial institutions. But his most relevant achievements are as a highly successful retail loan officer with personal mortgage production exceeding $250 million annually. Ken has also paid very close attention to other top loan officers and how they achieved their success, incorporating their most effective methods in his work and in this book.

Ken has been one of the industry's most active behind the scenes innovators. His efforts have directly changed HUD policies, established industry standards and created new loan products. His expertise has been recognized across the industry and he has been one of the few individuals to serve as a featured speaker at the annual conventions of the National Association of Home Builders, the Mortgage Bankers Association of America, and the National Association of Realtors®.

INTRODUCTION
REQUIRED READING

Mortgage banking can be a highly satisfying, financially rewarding, career-long profession. Like a "financial social worker," the position allows you the opportunity to help people with one of their largest investments while providing you with the potential of earning a very substantial income. What you will learn here is how to become a highly skilled mortgage banking practitioner so that you can convert that potential income into real income.

The most important advice for getting the most from this book is to read the entire book. The information contained here is provided in layers upon which you can build in order to extract the maximum benefit. If the reading seems less than stimulating, keep in mind that this book was written by a mortgage banker, not a novelist writing a steamy, make-believe adventure story. What you read here is the insight of someone who has successfully done the job, achieved the results and is now offering you the benefit of his experience and that of other highly successful mortgage bankers. If you are looking for excitement, that part comes when you apply the lessons offered here and your business volume and income skyrocket.

Before you begin, there are a few clarifications that should be proffered. First of all this is not a book on the technical aspects of mortgage finance. It doesn't address product knowledge such as LTV's, debt ratios or credit scores. Nor does it dwell on sales techniques, although it does address some pertinent sales skills directly related to mortgage business development. The focus of this book is on identifying potential business sources and cultivating them into long term, mutually beneficial business relationships. This book is about marketing yourself, your company and your services so that you can successfully capture a very large market share.

In mortgage banking there are essentially four things that are critical to your success. First you must have a full and complete understanding of all the loan products offered by your firm as well as the full range of Fannie Mae and Freddie Mac conventional loans. You must also have a comprehensive understanding of FHA and VA financing as well as USDA rural development financing if your market has a rural segment. A solid understanding of jumbo loans is essential as that is the realm where many successful loan officers dwell and prosper.

The second factor essential to success is your finely honed sales skill. Whether developed through books, seminars or any other media, highly refined sales techniques help you build strong personal business relationships with prospective borrowers and the referral sources upon which your professional mortgage banking practice is dependent.

Can you learn about loan products and build your sales skills "on the fly" as you pursue business? No! Certainly your skill in both areas will grow over time as you build your business, but you will be effectively shooting yourself in the foot by making sale calls prematurely.

Prospective referral sources, particularly real estate agents, will immediately recognize a lack of product knowledge and will write you off as an unskilled loan officer who can be of little value to them. First impressions are indelible. If you make a bad first impression it may take a very long time, if ever, to overcome that initial negative perception of your skill.

You will also need top level sales skills to build your relationships with referral sources, as real estate agents in particular, rely on your sales skills to help them cement the sale and build the agent's relationship with prospective buyers.

The third element that is essential to your success comes after you have built your product knowledge and refined your sales skills. That element is marketing. The marketing process entails identifying your prospective borrowers and referral sources and then presenting yourself, your company and the services that you offer in the most favorable light. Marketing is at the heart of this book.

Most loan officers have a basic understanding of loan products and their underwriting guidelines and many also have some basic sales skills, but that really isn't enough. Success requires stellar product knowledge and highly refined sales skills along with a powerful marketing plan.

The final critical factor is "doing it;" this is something this book can't teach you. You must supply your own motivation and initiative to take the information you will learn here and apply it to your business. You will need to work hard and sacrifice much to achieve that success, but that is true in any business or profession. But once you know what to do, the rest is easy. If you apply that knowledge appropriately you can convert it into high loan volume and an exceptional income.

It has been said that motivation comes from within, not from some external source. The realization that you have the knowledge necessary to become successful can be very motivating. It is frustrating to have the drive to achieve lofty goals without knowing the exact steps to create that optimal success. The lack of that knowledge is what causes many loan officers to flounder and ultimately fail.

Achieving success in mortgage banking, as well as most other things in life, is similar to standing on a beach and seeing an island on the horizon that represents success. You know what success should be and you can vaguely see it from where you are, but you simply can't figure out how to get there. This book will show you the way.

Many people will attend motivational seminars and then go back to the same job, performing the same duties in the same way. Before long, the motivation and energy generated by the speaker will have faded. If you aren't getting the results you want then you must change what you are doing. Einstein described insanity as doing the same thing over and over and expecting different results.

Here, you will learn to do things differently, to do things right and to achieve spectacular results. That will stimulate your motivation; no insanity required.

This book will certainly reiterate some familiar suggestions, but you will also be exposed to many new ways to identify and generate business from both obvious and obscure sources. It has been said that the best way to become successful in your chosen field is to find someone who has achieved optimum success and then do exactly what they do. That doesn't mean do some of the things they do, it means do all the things they do in exactly the same way they do them.

Far too many people look at what successful people do and think that they can duplicate their success by doing just some of the things that the successful person does and not bother with the part that looks like it will be unpleasant. The reality is that those unpleasant tasks are what make the difference. Those are the things your competitors don't want to do either. But they are exactly what needs to be done to achieve extraordinary success. It is the difference between exactly following the recipe for a gourmet meal to make it perfect or choosing to leave out some of the ingredients because they seem minor or are expensive or would require an extra trip to the grocery store.

Success comes from using not just some of the ingredients but using each and every ingredient in the right proportion because, as in every other aspect of life, it is the little things that make the difference. And mortgage banking is just like that gourmet meal, where you must read the recipe and gather all the ingredients so that the execution of the recipe is flawless. In other words, create a business plan comprised of all the elements described in this book, organize each of the components and then execute with precision.

Throughout this book you will hear the same message over and over. It is more than the ramblings of a loquacious author it is an effort to instill in you the importance of the message.

After reading this book (every word of every chapter) you will not only know what to do, but you will know exactly how to do it (no shortcuts allowed).

Hopefully you will build a personal business plan along the way to incorporate each of the tasks essential to your success. Draw on all the ideas presented here and build a strong, comprehensive plan around them because it is not just a case of doing some of the little things, it is a case of consistently doing all the little things to achieve success. And don't forget the big things too.

Then, if it is helpful to you, attend a motivational seminar to raise your energy level and build your excitement, because when you emerge from the event, you will not only be energized, but you will know exactly where you are going and how to get there. But, by then you may not need the motivational speaker, because by knowing how to mine all the gold in mortgage banking, your motivation can come from within.

By following the roadmap laid out in this book, you will have all the tools to build an extraordinary mortgage banking practice that can produce exceptional business volume and the phenomenal income that follows. It is simply a question of whether you choose to follow the advice presented here and make the sacrifices that are essential to achieving success.

Before you can effectively apply the knowledge you will gather from this book it is of critical importance that you have exceedingly strong product knowledge and highly refined sales skills. Without those capabilities, the business development and marketing techniques presented in this book are worthless.

It is said that the shortest distance between two points is a straight line. But more importantly, the longest distance is the short cut. Every time you try to skip some of the steps in a process or leave out some of the details, you may find that things don't work out and you have to go back and do it again the right way. By the time you are finished you have probably used much more time and energy than you would have used had you done it right the first time. There are no short cuts; not in mortgage banking and not in life. Do it all and do it right. Pay attention, follow the roadmap and reap the rewards.

Chapter 1
First Things First

Mortgage Banking is an excellent vehicle for achieving high personal and financial success. It offers unlimited income, prestige, flexibility and never ending challenges. But, the competition is fierce and survival of the fittest applies with a vengeance. You must be prepared to compete with formidable opposition and be tenacious enough to persevere when faced with what will appear to be insurmountable obstacles. Those challenges are what will also discourage your competitors and allow you to achieve phenomenal success.

In the chapters that follow, you will learn, step by step, how to achieve the highest goals in mortgage banking. These guidelines can also be modified to fit many other professions, but since we are focusing on mortgage banking, we will assume that is the means you have chosen to achieve your goals.

The business development methods presented in this book can be the vital difference to the success of any enterprising mortgage loan officer as they have been for a select few of the most successful mortgage loan officers in America. The level of success you attain is up to you, but it is directly related to your level of knowledge and skill combined with the amount of effort and sacrifice you are willing to put forth to achieve your objectives. While this book provides all the information you will need to attain optimum results from your effort, you must apply that knowledge with a substantial consistent commitment of time, energy and efficiency. The bottom line is that the book will tell you what to do, but it is up to you to do it.

If you follow the ideas presented in this book you should dramatically improve your effectiveness and generate maximum return on your effort. But you must do more than read and understand the ideas; they must be implemented. And, because they have been gleaned from the techniques used by many of the nation's most successful mortgage loan officers, there are more ideas than a loan officer may reasonably use. Of course the objective is to provide you with as many options as possible to let you develop a marketing plan that suits you and your market. However, no matter what methods you use, no one achieves maximum success without maximum effort.

If you are unable or unwilling to commit a minimum of ten to twelve hours per day to any sales position, and mortgage banking is most certainly sales, then you should reconsider your career objectives. Your true level of success should be judged by your achievements when compared with the goals you have personally set for yourself. You also need to remember that your success in the eyes of others is determined by how you compare with your peers. If you work only as hard as most of them you will probably achieve similar results, making you an average performer. To be above average, a star performer, you must commit to working smarter and working harder. You must determine which efforts produce the best return; then decide which of those efforts are most compatible with your talents and personality. You then need to "compress" the time frame normally needed to perform those tasks by removing the superfluous activities and concentrating on those which produce the highest return on your effort.

If you have a tendency to procrastinate, it can be minimized by building a tight business plan, then, as the old adage goes, plan your work and work your plan. If you do that, you will not have time to procrastinate; you will simply have to put procrastination off until another day. It may also help you to understand that most people who procrastinate do so by pushing everything that needs to be done closer to the deadline so that they then have too little time to complete the job in a high quality manner. It becomes their excuse for doing sub-standard work. Since you will be doing everything at the highest level of quality, there will be no need for excuses because your performance should be near perfect.

To demonstrate the destructive power of procrastination, think in terms of putting off only ten percent of your tasks each work day. If you work a twelve hour day, over a period of a year, you will have wasted more than a full month of time. If there is a month differential between the amount of work you do compared to that of a competitor, who do you think is going to be more successful? Even if the issue isn't fighting with a competitor for the top spot, you need to recognize that time wasted is opportunity lost and money not earned.

Even if you decide that you are not willing to commit twelve hours per day, it is essential to understand that you need to get the most accomplished in the time that you allocate. Some people will put in eight, ten or twelve hours a day, but by wasting a large portion of that time they may have put in the equivalent of only three or four hours of effective work. If you only want to put in four hours per day, make them highly effective and productive hours and take the rest of the day off. If you are going to spend eight hours or twelve hours on your work, don't let those be empty hours, make them full, productive hours. Don't sit around putting in the hours without putting in the work. It isn't the hours that produce business, it is the work. The results will make it very clear to everyone, just how hard you really are working. High achievement fosters even greater achievement. And you earn lots of money.

Most people start out their career with the intent of being successful. Very few, however, actually achieve the degree of success they originally hoped for. This is because most people have only a vague idea of what they want to achieve. They think of success only in the most general of terms. They may think of a certain dollar amount they would like to earn each year or a specific amount of assets they would like to possess or perhaps a position they would like to occupy. However, with most people, these things are mere "wants." If asked, most people will surely say that they would "like" to be a millionaire. But while they would like to be a millionaire, very few actually have the true desire and willingness to do the work and make the sacrifices to achieve the level of accomplishment that produces true wealth.

To truly desire something, you must be willing to take all the steps and make all the sacrifices necessary to achieve that goal. Every worthwhile achievement will have formidable obstacles to overcome and significant sacrifices to be made before the goal is reached.   These are the things that keep people from great achievements.   It is these obstacles that separate the mundane, valueless goals from the achievements which have high value, in terms of dollars and recognition.   Simply put, anyone can accomplish the objectives that require little work or sacrifice and have correspondingly little value, but it takes the person with exceptional determination and perseverance to achieve the extraordinary goals.   The good news is that it is within everyone's reach.

Giving up is easy, and the majority of the population will choose that route when things get difficult.   They take the easy way and end up settling for mediocrity.   That is why very few people actually reach the lofty goals to which they aspire; most people give up too soon because the obstacles appear too formidable for them and give them an excuse to take a less arduous path.   The few who succeed don't accept these barriers as too difficult to overcome. They realize that all obstacles can be conquered in one way or another.

When humans desired to fly, they didn't give up simply because flapping their arms didn't achieve the desired results; they built balloons, kites, airplanes and rockets to propel them through the air.   These methods were not what mankind first envisioned when he desired to fly, but they were the results of his willingness to use alternative methods rather than standing there flapping his arms and hoping to fly.   This same principle applies to all things in life, including mortgage banking.   The choice is yours; flap your arms or build a rocket.

Chapter 2
Sacrifice

It is important to recognize and fully understand what you will need to do to achieve success as a mortgage banker. An essential element is acknowledging that success comes with a price. Whether your objective is financial success or having a happy, satisfying and well rounded personal and family relationship, you must make some sacrifices.

The sad reality is that there are only 168 hours in each week. On the bright side, your competitors have exactly the same amount of time. Everything you do uses some of that time; whether it is eating, sleeping, working or doing some of the things you enjoy with your friends or family. So, the more time you focus on your work, the less time there will be left for your family and the other activities that you enjoy. The opposite is true as well; the more time you dedicate to your family and fun activities, the fewer hours that you will have available for your work.

There is always some sacrifice because you simply can't create more hours in the week. John Randolph said, "Time is at once the most valuable and the most perishable of all our possessions." By instilling balance in your work and personal life with judicious use of your time you can achieve phenomenal success. But, it happens by design, not by chance. You need a business and personal plan to guide you.

One of the appealing aspects about a career in mortgage banking is the flexibility it offers to mortgage loan officers. This is a job that can be successfully mastered by working only half of each day. What is even more important is that it doesn't matter whether you choose the first twelve hours, the last twelve hours or twelve hours somewhere in the middle. But, be very clear, you will need to plan on working a minimum of twelve full hours each day or about 60 or more hours per week. That doesn't mean sitting in your office doing nothing for twelve hours every day and then going home without accomplishing anything. It means twelve hours of intensely focused, highly compressed and extremely productive activities directly related to building and servicing your clientele. Besides, the guy who sits in his office doing nothing for twelve hours consumes the same amount of time as the loan officer who works hard for twelve productive hours; the difference is in the paycheck. If you are going to put in the time; get value for the time you invest.

There are no miracle solutions that will magically create high production and a soaring income. You will actually be required to work hard. There is no magic wand that you can wave that will produce miraculous results. You must make an extraordinary effort. But this book will show you more and better ways so that every aspect of your effort pays off with a far greater return. And, if you are starting to think that maybe you don't have to do all this work, that maybe if you just loiter in the office that you will be lucky and business will simply come to you, perish the thought. If you are depending on luck remember the old adage that says "the harder you work, the luckier you get." When you work hard and work smart amazing things happen.

In mortgage banking you will cultivate a broad spectrum of resources from which you can generate business. Some will be individuals who are direct sources of business, but most will be individuals who are in a position to refer multiple clients to you. These sources with referral capability represent the best way to leverage your efforts and create more income.

As you work your way through this book, make a list of things to do each day. Start building a business plan that includes your business and personal activities because they are all part of the same plan. Don't tie most of them to a specific time of the day because you probably already know that a call from a prospective borrower or referral source can quickly change your schedule. However you can include many activities in an early morning block of time and others in an evening block of time. There are things that need to be accomplished each and every day in order to achieve realistic goals but flexibility is essential. For now, it needs to be a very changeable business plan because it will probably be adjusted many times before you get to the end of this book.

You will find a suggested weekly work plan in Chapter 26 that you can use as a guideline, but it is just a framework that you can use to build your personal business plan. When you have finished reading this book, it will be your responsibility to craft all the ideas into a workable plan that is custom designed to fit your preferred way of working. You must have a written plan because it serves as your roadmap to success; no map, no success.

Chapter 3
The Fundamentals

There is no easy way to achieve success, but there are certain ways to optimize your activities so that success is achieved in the most efficient manner possible. And, unfortunately, there are many ways to undermine your hard work as well. If you are going to put in the hours and do all the work, you also want maximum results for your efforts.

Sometimes, no matter how diligent you are at performing all the tasks that are described in these chapters, some loan officers will not get stellar results.

In this chapter, these issues will be faced head-on, giving some loan officers the cold slap of reality that they need to wake them up. Once conscious, they can extract the maximum benefits from their efforts. You may recognize that you already understand and adhere to these guidelines so you can simply sit back and know that you are already doing things the right way. Sure, some loan officers will probably be insulted and assert that these things really aren't important. Of course, that will also explain their abysmal production volume.

These points are not intended to insult anyone, but to help everyone. Sometimes, we slip into a mode of behavior that is counterproductive without realizing it. We don't think about some of the things that we do simply because they are the things we have always done. In some instances those things you have done are exactly the things that you should not do. In other cases there are things that you may not have done that you absolutely need to do. This chapter simply puts these things in perspective.

You have already heard that it will take a lot of work, including about sixty hours of focused activities every week. All that activity requires a lot of energy. The most certain way to raise your energy level is to raise your fitness level. If you are overweight or out of shape, this is the time to get fit. Regular exercise, whether it is swimming, bicycling, running, playing tennis, aerobics, racquetball, working out at the health club or a vigorous walk each day will help you in more ways than you can imagine.

When you are out of shape, you are likely to be lethargic even though you may not even realize it, and that lack of energy can dilute your motivation and prevent you from completing all the tasks that are ahead of you each day. When you are fit, you simply feel better, think more clearly and the higher metabolism that results from regular workouts gives you the energy to achieve far more than you are likely to accomplish while in couch potato mode.

Since we are not talking about preparing for world class athletic competition, a modest, but regular fitness program will suffice. For most people, working out three times per week will be adequate. The hard part is getting started and adhering to a fitness program. Your new fitness plan should become a lifelong program that becomes easier as you integrate it into your regular schedule so that it becomes part of your daily routine. Using the facilities of a gym or health club has the added benefit of creating another networking venue.

If you have not been engaged in a regular exercise program, the very first thing you need to do is consult with your personal physician and be certain that you don't have any detectible health impairment that may put you at risk from a change in exercise and or diet. Any time you raise your heart rate you will be stressing your body so you need to start slow. Begin by walking a mile or two a couple of days each week for a few weeks before your start to run or bicycle. Even then, take it easy at first because you are trying to improve your health, not kill yourself. Also keep in mind that these activities are simply to improve your fitness level, not prepare you for competitive athletic events.

Far too many people fail to understand that they are preparing their body to work longer and harder, not compete in the Iron Man Triathlon. Some people simply use poor judgment by trying to get into shape the first day and do way too much. These people are generally described by the medical profession as the deceased. The survivors are divided between the fit and successful and those who give up their workout because they try to do too much too soon and the pain has discouraged them from continuing.

William Shakespeare said in his play "As You Like It" that "All the world is a stage, and all the men and women merely players." The point for us being, that in our career we are playing the role of a mortgage banker. If you were producing a movie and had a character designated as a successful, intelligent, prosperous mortgage banker, how would this person act? How would they dress? What manners and mannerisms would they exhibit and what other characteristics would be applied to this person?

Your clients and referral sources will have certain expectations and perception about the qualities that they believe a mortgage banker should possess. Most of them think of a mortgage lender as a banker. Consequently, they expect a mortgage banker to look and act like a banker or at least the stereotypical banker, like the one you would cast in your movie.

Your friends may refer prospective borrowers to you because they know you and because they think you are competent and a person of integrity; or it may be that they refer business to you because you are the only mortgage banker they know. The reality is that they are unlikely to expect the person that they refer to you to refer other business back to them, nor are they likely to have a commission check riding on your success with that borrower. Consequently, your friend's criteria for choosing or recommending a mortgage lender is quite different from an accountant, lawyer, financial planner, real estate agent or any of the other potential referral sources we will discuss. Regardless of the motivation for your friend's referrals, you should still cultivate them as potential sources of direct and referral business.

When someone refers a client to you in a professional environment, they know that your performance and professionalism will be a direct reflection on them. Even if they know that you are the smartest, most competent mortgage banker in town, they simply will not risk sending a valued client to you if you do not represent the highest standards of what a mortgage banker should be. If you are rude, use inappropriate language, dress like a slob or have the energy level of a sloth, you don't even need to bother getting off the couch to try to get some of the business that professionals could refer to you. Only those prospective referral sources with the lowest self-esteem would risk their professional reputation and their paycheck by referring business to anyone but a top tier mortgage banker.

Consider something that many loan officers may regard as trite. Certainly, there has been a trend toward dressing more casually than business people did in the past. However, there are two important things to recognize. The first is that the trend toward casual business dress reversed itself and the move is now back toward the classic business attire; the second is that there is a direct measurable correlation between how you dress and the amount of business you can expect to generate. The better you dress (not in a tux, please), the more professional and successful you appear. Remember, perception is reality. If you are thought to be successful, then it will be assumed that your success is a result of your competence and business skill. More business will therefore be referred to you, making you even more successful and causing the spiral to continue to rise until you are achieving all your goals. Play the role, dress the part and soon you will be the role model for the professional mortgage banker.

If you are skeptical of what is being recommended, put yourself in the position of a real estate agent where you have a choice of referring a client to two loan officers; one always dressed neatly in a conservative dark business suit, starched white shirt and attractive conservative tie while the other always wears an old stained t-shirt, cut-off jeans and flip-flops. Which one would you choose? Even if both loan officers were of equal competence, to which loan officer would you choose to risk your commission check, reputation and future referrals from the client?

Your immediate reaction would probably be that no loan officer would dress in cut-offs and an old t-shirt. You would probably be right. But the question remains, if these were the only two choices that you had, which loan officer would you choose? Let us hope that you would have enough sense to choose the loan officer that is properly dressed in a nice suit, white shirt and tie because that is the choice your referral sources will make. When professional referral sources choose which mortgage loan officer to whom they will refer a client, they have to make a similar decision.

Of course, the distinction between loan officer choices may not be quite so stark, but the question remains: if a referral source is more likely to choose the mortgage banker in a suit than the guy in the t-shirt, aren't they also more likely to choose someone in a suit rather than someone in Dockers and a golf shirt? The answer is probably "yes," unless you happen to work in a golf or beach community, where everyone tends to dress more casually. But, even there you need to think of one thing: which loan officer looks more professional? Which one looks more like the banker? Which one is more likely to stand out from their competitors? Which one is more like the person you would have cast in your movie to play the part of the professional, successful mortgage banker?

Dress for success is more than a vague theory. There have been comprehensive studies conducted that confirm the validity of dressing appropriately to the job you are doing. Consumers want their doctor to look like a doctor; their gardener to look like a gardener; their plumber to look like a plumber, and their mortgage banker to look like a banker. This generally means a starched and pressed white shirt not a purple shirt; it means an attractive, conservative tie that is properly tied and drawn up to the buttoned collar and a conservative business suit.

Although you may see men on TV wearing a purple shirt or a shirt of another color, remember that they are in the entertainment industry, not in the banking business. For a reference, look at the web site for any major bank and see how their senior officers and directors are dressed in their photos. Appearances aren't everything, but unless the appearances are appropriate, the client will never bother to learn how competent you are. This also applies to your casual attire on weekends or while you are on errands around the community. Jeans, shorts or other casual clothes are fine if they are neat and clean and appropriate for the activity in which you are engaged. But don't ever go out in a sweat suit as no one looks good in one. You never know when you are going to encounter a prospective client or referral source.

Appropriateness goes both ways. A close friend who was a very successful mortgage banker and a skilled salesman had a brother who was a building contractor that specialized in building patios and room additions. The brother had placed an ad in the local newspaper advertising patios at a very attractive price. The ad drew so many calls that the contractor couldn't get to everyone but he also didn't want to lose the potential business.

As brothers often do, the mortgage banker jumped in to help by going to see some of the homeowners in the evening to prepare estimates and hopefully sign contracts for the new patios. After several days of sales calls, usually seeing two or three homeowners each evening, the mortgage banker hadn't sold a single patio while his contractor brother was signing up an average of two people every evening. The mortgage banker couldn't understand how his brother, who was not a polished salesman, was outselling him.

One evening, after stopping at home to eat a quick dinner before heading out for his three appointments that evening, the mortgage banker stopped at the front door to straighten his tie in a mirror. It was in that moment he realized he was not dressed appropriately for what he was selling. He quickly changed into some khaki slacks, a denim work shirt and clean work boots. He sold all three prospects a patio that evening. The problem hadn't been his sales skills, nor had it been the quality of his attire. The problem was that he was not dressed appropriately.

When dressed in his suit, the homeowners he visited likely assumed that he was a commissioned salesman working for the contractor. Even at the low price that was being quoted they must have assumed they were still paying too much or the quality would be low if the contractor was making enough to pay salesmen. But, when he looked like a contractor, he was more believable for the role he was playing. Be believable for the role you are playing, dress like a professional, successful, competent mortgage banker.

The bottom line is that you have a choice of dressing the very best way you can or choosing something less. Every time you choose to do anything in any but the very best possible way you are giving away business and diluting the effect of all your business development efforts. If you are going to do the work, reap the maximum reward. Do everything the very best way possible and receive the maximum amount of business that you have already earned.

Now that we have dressed you up, can we take you out? The answer depends on several other factors. Everyone needs to be freshly showered and groomed. Don't forget deodorant, teeth brushed, flossed and mouth wash. This means that men need to shave and not try to emulate the three day shadow unless for reasons of religious belief it is appropriate to maintain facial hair. But even then, it should be very neatly groomed. Men should avoid facial hair at all cost unless they feel the need to minimize a facial characteristic. A neatly trimmed moustache is usually acceptable, but anything more than that will absolutely diminish your business success.

Some loan officers have suggested that since I am older, that my suggestions of how someone should dress are vestiges of a different generation. The truth is that I would rather wear jeans and a comfortable shirt than a suit and starched white shirt, but I have seen the studies and I know there is a very big difference in how clients perceive a mortgage banker based on how they dress. I have also heard the feed-back from clients and referral sources. They expect a mortgage loan officer to look like a banker otherwise things just don't look right.

Virtually all of the male loan officers that earn a seven figure income dress in dark business suits, starched white shirts, or occasionally the traditional light blue shirt or predominately white shirts with pin stripes and cuff links, a colorful but conservative tie and polished black shoes. Female loan officers wear equivalent attire which may consist of a conservative suit that is always tasteful and of course they wear hose and nice closed toe pumps with modest heels. Skirts are of moderate length, although some will wear upscale slacks with a coordinated jacket. Clothing should never be excessively tight or overly revealing at the neckline, midriff or legs.

The image that successful male and female mortgage bankers project is one of competence and professionalism. The attention that they apply to their wardrobe and grooming conveys a clear message that they pay very close attention to the details, something that is critically important in a loan officer.

By now you may be thinking that you aren't going to conform to someone else's idea of how a loan officer should dress; that you feel that you have the right to show your individuality and dress any way you choose. Certainly you have a choice, but the choice you make will directly affect the amount of business that you generate. If you make a poor choice your competitors will appreciate all the business they are receiving because you have chosen to wear an inappropriate outfit for a mortgage banker. If you were given the role in a movie as a mortgage banker, you would certainly wear the appropriate "costume," so why not play the role of a successful mortgage banker in real life?

Among the small, but not insignificant issues that you will address as a mortgage banker is the matter of Realtors®. The important point here is that all Realtors® are licensed real estate agents, brokers or appraisers, but not all agents, brokers, or appraisers are Realtors® despite the fact that many people use the term "REALTOR®" as a synonym for "real estate agent."

The term "REALTOR®" is a registered trademark of the National Association of REALTORS® (NAR) and only their members may use that term to describe themselves. Some agents and brokers are extremely sensitive about how the term is used and often use it as a litmus test of loan officers to determine whether they really understand their business. So, here is an important rule, don't refer to anyone as a Realtor® but simply refer to real estate agents as "agents" and brokers as "brokers." That way you won't misspeak.

When you write the term "REALTOR®" or "REALTORS®" the word should be in upper case, but it is also acceptable to use lower case as long as you capitalize the "R" at the beginning of the word and place the "®" after the word. While some Realtors® don't care about the proper usage and others don't know what is correct, you need to get it right every time. Like any other factor, doing it wrong can cost you business.

The National Association of REALTORS® has modified trademark rules for domain names, email addresses and Internet usage in general. For an explanation of all the permitted and prohibited uses you may review the trademark rules on the NAR website at:
"http://www.realtor.org/letterlw.nsf/pages/trademarkmanual."

The most useful parts of the manual are Part One, Section IV (Limitations on usage); Part Two, Section III (Internet usage) and Part Three, Section III (Uses to avoid). But, feel free to read all the rules; it can't hurt.

One other thing to remember: the word REALTOR® has only two syllables and is pronounced "Real-tor." Too often people try to add an additional syllable in the middle. As one broker said "you wouldn't say "doc-a-tor" so why would you say "Real-a-tor?" Once you know the proper usage you will see lots of violations by agents and brokers alike. Don't bother to point them out. Remember, this is a sales job, so you need to know to do all the right things and do none of the wrong things. You don't gain favor by correcting anyone else's behavior, and always remember the commission check a Realtor® referral may generate.

Chapter 4
General Rules for Business & Life

There are some rules that apply to every aspect of your life. You are probably aware of most of them and some of the most obvious aren't even discussed here. However, there are a few rules that are worthy of mention.

Never speak negatively of anyone, no matter how big a jerk they may be. While other people may say unflattering things about your competitors or your referral sources or members of Congress or any number of people, simply let them talk without agreeing or disagreeing with them. If you must respond, give a neutral reply by simply saying something like "I understand" or "I know how you feel." Don't get pushed into a corner. Even if you do agree with them, don't say so because they may tell other people what you said. If those people don't agree with you, that may weaken your business opportunities with them. When the opportunity presents itself, move on to another topic.

If your position on matters is unknown, everyone will presume that you must agree with them, since you didn't argue with their point of view. In politics people are far more likely to vote against a candidate because of a position with which they disagree than vote in favor of a candidate with whom they do agree. You need to be certain that you have not provided the ammunition for someone to "vote" against doing business with you because of your position on an immaterial matter. And, it is always immaterial if it doesn't put business in your hand.

The problem with saying negative things is that your listeners may then presume that you may say negative things about them. They may also be concerned that someone will overhear your comments and inaccurately attribute the comments to them since they were a party to the conversation. They may disagree with you, but know better than to say so. As we well know, everyone has opinions; keep yours to yourself as it is difficult to disagree with someone whose opinion is unknown. Even when it relates to financial markets or mortgage products or other matters where your referral sources and clients look to you for your respected counsel, be very cautious.

There is an important rule that you may have heard before and it applies here as well as in other aspects of your life: Don't discuss religion, politics or sex and don't use profanity. This isn't being prudish, it's being smart. Even those people who use inappropriate language respect those who don't use it.

Avoid comments, or worse, commitments related to the direction mortgage rates may be moving, because as brilliant as you may be, it is virtually impossible to predict the future. If you tell someone rates may be headed down, and they fail to lock their rate before rates go up, you will probably be personally blamed for any loss they believe they have suffered.

Every borrower should be encouraged to lock their rate when they apply for their loan. If they question your recommendation, explain that rates tend to move upward much more rapidly than they move downward because bankers, being relatively conservative, try to stay ahead of the rate curve. Therefore, any gain the borrower may potentially receive if rates move lower is substantially offset by the greater risk that rates may move higher.

Any change in rates is likely to be minimal in the brief time between application and closing so it isn't worth worrying about movement in rates in that time frame. However, it is always the borrower's choice; be certain they understand that they need to make their decision based on whether they feel the possible gain from a potentially lower rate is worth the risk of the rates moving higher. Most lenders require the borrower to sign a document stating that they are choosing to "lock" or "float" the rate. You are encouraged to use such a document even if your employer does not require that it be used.

Occasionally, borrowers will ask you to call them if you "think" rates are going to move or if you are aware that your company's rates will change. Don't be put in this position by your borrower. Tell them that you become very busy when there are rumors of rate changes and that you can't accept the responsibility for notifying them when a change in rates seems apparent. If you are not available, you don't want them to lose an opportunity as a result.

Explain to the borrower that they have the option of assuming the risk of changes in the market, both up and down by allowing the rate to float or that they may transfer the risk to your company by locking-in the rate. You are in this business to make money so do not be put in a position where you could lose money or clients because the financial markets take a turn.

Whatever you do, don't "play the market." Do not tell a borrower that they are locked when they are not or conversely that their rate is floating when it is already locked. I have seen loan officers "play the market" this way, hoping to gain a greater rate spread and "overage" when the rates move. They usually lose a lot of money as well as their client and their job. If you want to make overage on a loan, build it in at the front end when you quote and lock rates. Just remember to follow your company's rules regarding overage as many large lenders no longer permit loan officers to charge overage.

In my career of more than forty years in mortgage banking, the only time that I was certain where rates were going was when two of my clients who had been floating the rate called within ten minutes of each other to lock their rate. What made this relevant is that they were both high ranking economists with different agencies of the federal government. I suspect that they knew something. In fact, rates did move higher that same day. However, without some similar inside source to give you a strong sense of where the market may be heading, don't take a chance on prognosticating interest rates. In fact, never do it because the only rates that you can accurately predict are yesterday's rates. You are a mortgage banker, not an economist or a psychic.

Chapter 5
Important Stuff

Now that I have lectured and whined about a lot of the pain in the butt minutia that you need to be aware of while performing your job as a mortgage banker, here are the important things that you really need to know.

To reiterate, you should now be out of your smelly old t-shirt and cut-offs and into a professional suit. You should look good, smell good or best of all have no discernible fragrance at all and you know about the Realtors® trademark. You know never to speak negatively of anyone, to stay silent in debates and never to speculate about the direction of interest rates. Hopefully you also know about loan programs and have cultivated your sales skills.

You may be experienced as a loan officer, but we are still going to start at the very beginning because many of those reading this book may be new to the profession. Even for the seasoned mortgage banker, it is good to refresh your memory. You may even pick up a few new ideas or remember some you have forgotten.
Here are some important considerations:

1.   What is your title? You are not a mortgage solicitor or loan originator. Those and similar titles make it sound like you are the "mortgage pimp" and work on a street corner. When anyone asks or you volunteer what you do for a profession, tell them that you are a "Mortgage Banker." After all that is what you are. You always need to market yourself in the most positive light and in surveys bankers tend to rank near the top as being trustworthy.

Of course, we are all really loan officers, but to the public you need to be viewed as a mortgage banker.

2.   Make certain that your employer uses a proper title for you on your business cards. Yes, it is fine if they want to call you a Loan Officer or Mortgage Banker, but absolutely not an "originator" or "solicitor" or some other demeaning or derogatory title. Titles are marketing tools; use them to your best advantage. If the company doesn't want to use an appropriate title, then suggest that they simply use no title at all. The worst situation is to have a title that degrades what you do.

3.   You don't work "for" anyone. You are "with" XYZ Mortgage Company. This is a subtle difference, but it elevates you from a subservient position to one of equality in the organization. Prospective clients want to work with someone who has some stature in an organization because it implies skill and competence. You will never hear an attorney say that they work for Smith & Jones but rather they are with Smith & Jones. Most professionals use the phrase indicating that they are "with" a firm rather than working "for" someone.

4.   Explain the subtle differences mentioned above to your spouse or other significant person in your life. Also tell your children how they should refer to you and the work you do and the importance of how you are perceived. With children, don't explain the alternative that you are trying to supplant as they will give people the entire explanation that you are "a mortgage banker not a loan solicitor, etc." Kids are cute, but they are parrots and repeat all that they hear. Be certain that your "ambassadors" represent you well and describe you as a professional mortgage banker.

5.   Wear a name tag. Now you are probably whining that you don't like name tags. Trust me, they are worth it. When you don't wear a name tag, people simply don't know who you are. You may think that you are famous in every real estate office in town but the truth is that you are probably not; at least not yet. We will get you there. Wear your name tag on your lapel on the right side of your suit. It is more visible there to the people you meet. Be certain the name is the way you want to be referred. If your name is Robert Smith but you prefer to be called "Bob" then your name tag should use "Bob Smith" along with the name of your company. Don't bother to include a title as name tags need to be easy to read and brevity helps. You need to be absolutely certain that everyone you meet knows who you are and wearing a name tag doesn't just make a difference, it make a huge difference.

If you prefer, you can remove the name tag when you are away from the real estate agent's office, but you never know how many people in the grocery store will see the name tag and notice that you are a mortgage banker; they just may be in the market to buy or refinance a home. When meeting with other professional referral sources where your contact is more likely with just one person such as an attorney or accountant, the name tag is optional and it can be put in a pocket because it is not essential. If you give the person your business card, that is sufficient.

A good example related to name tags is physicians in a hospital; virtually everyone wears a name tag because they encounter a lot of patients, staff and others who need to know who they are. On the other hand, doctors in private practice, attorneys and accountants rarely wear name tags because they see people in a more controlled environment where everyone is likely to know who they are.

Admittedly, name tags can be a small detraction from the highly professional image that you want to project. However, if you have the choice of being dapper or being the mortgage banker that prospective clients and referral sources can identify, go with the latter. Of course you still need to wear that professional suit but now you need to accessorize it with the name tag. It's not too much of a compromise.

When in the office of any referral source, be certain to give a couple of your business cards to each person you encounter including the professional and clerical staff. They may know someone who needs a mortgage or they may personally need financing. Never miss an opportunity to introduce yourself to people and to let them know that you are a mortgage banker who can help them or people they know obtain a mortgage.

As your business volume increases, you will find that the distribution of tasks you perform will change. In the early stages when you have very few loans in process, you can spend nearly all your time making sales calls, presenting seminars and networking. Over the years, as your production begins to reflect your earlier sales effort, you will have less time for personal sales calls on prospective clients and will make more contact with what will then be your established accounts by phone, email or brief handwritten notes. You will then need to spend more time in your office taking phone calls from referral sources and prospective clients and meeting with potential borrowers.

Chapter 6
Attitude & Motivation

The first step in overcoming obstacles and achieving your objectives is having the proper attitude. While this may sound clichéd, it is extremely important. It may, in fact be one of the most important factors in determining whether you achieve the success you desire.

Your attitude not only sets the tenor for your actions, but also is the cue for other people's reactions. It is, therefore, important that you not only have a good attitude, but that other people perceive your attitude as positive. Without question, people want to be around other individuals with a very positive outlook and most importantly for our purposes, they want to conduct business with people who have a positive perspective.

There is no question that if a real estate agent is given a choice of two loan officers of equal skill with whom to conduct business, they will select the one that has the positive approach. They want a loan officer who looks at how a borrower can be approved, rather than dwelling on the negative aspects of an application. This is not to say that you should neglect the negative points of a borrower's application but speak to the positive aspects. The successful mortgage banker always looks for ways to approve loans because you don't get paid for loans that never close.

Attitude can have a genetic origin, but it can also be an issue of cause-and-effect. People respond to us in relation to their perception of us. If we are positive and up-beat, then they will generally react accordingly. If we project a negative attitude, then their response to us will likely be negative. Of course injecting an element of humor can take the cold edge off a negative business situation and add a little warmth so that it becomes more personal. The combination of knowledge, attitude and personal warmth with a little humor can build great relationships, both business and personal.

William James, the father of Psychology in America stated "human beings can change their lives by altering their attitudes and minds." In essence, he is stating that our minds control our lives, and we have the opportunity to take control of our lives by programming our minds to reflect a positive, success oriented life. And, when you meet with that occasional set back, do not focus on it, but learn from it then set it aside and move forward, putting your emphasis once again on the positive aspects of what you seek to accomplish.

Life is simply a mirror reflecting what we project. Everything we receive from life will be a direct reflection of our attitude and our effort. When we project a positive attitude the results will generally be positive. If we display a negative attitude, the results may correspond.

Having an image as a person who approaches life in a positive, up-beat manner, will draw people toward you. It will help you develop a broad range of personal friendships. It is these personal relationships that direct business your way. Someone once said that people will cross the street to talk with someone who is friendly, positive and offers genuine compliments. They will cross the street even more quickly to avoid a person who projects negativity. Which person are you? Which person is likely to get referrals? When someone has the opportunity to refer a prospective borrower to a mortgage banker who do you think they will choose?

Chapter 7
Knowledge is Power

A real estate agent will never call you unless they believe you have the answers that can solve their problems. Answers come from product knowledge and experience. Only time can give you experience, but the more effort that is expended in gaining knowledge, the less time that will be required to obtain the experience.

Success is a process that develops from knowledge of your products, knowledge of your competitors, knowledge of the products offered by your competitors, knowledge of the real estate sales agents and the brokerage firms with whom they are associated, knowledge of each of your other referral sources and most importantly, knowledge of yourself. If you do not understand your capabilities and limits, as well as your objectives and reasons for seeking these objectives, it will be far more difficult for you to achieve your goals.

While success is a process, you can ill afford to step into the office of a referral source with anything less than maximum preparation. It does not matter how smart you become next week or next month. If the agent's first impression is that you have a poor knowledge of mortgage lending it may be a long time before you can change that image. First impressions are indelible, so be certain you are prepared to imprint an exemplary image in the eyes of everyone you meet.

So, where do you obtain all this valuable knowledge that is so essential to success? Unfortunately, some of it really does take time and experience because many of the situations you will face in your career will not surface in your first week in the business. Aside from time and experience, one of the best ways to build your product knowledge is the Seller and Servicer guides from the Federal National Mortgage Association (Fannie Mae) and the Federal Home Loan Mortgage Corporation (Freddie Mac). Because these organizations are the two largest buyers of conventional mortgages, most loans are structured and underwritten to their standards.

For government loans, the guidelines set by the Federal Housing Administration (FHA) and the Veterans Administration (VA) will need to be studied. It is also important that you look to the directives of the local FHA and VA offices that have jurisdiction over the market in which you originate business. The guidelines of each office are often slightly different. This is also true of the regional underwriting offices for Fannie Mae and Freddie Mac. If your market area includes rural properties, then you also need to read the guidelines for the United States Department of Agriculture (USDA) Rural Development Loans.

The next reference source is the mortgage product descriptions of the loans offered by your company. It is essential that you fully understand these programs so that you can explain them to real estate agents and borrowers. You must also be able to compare and contrast your offerings with those of your competitors. This is not as easy as it once was due to the vast number of mortgage programs and the proliferation of loan brokering. Both have allowed companies to offer a seemingly endless assortment of loans. It has also meant that they can change from day to day and keeping track of those product changes can be very challenging. However, most loans are rooted in the Fannie Mae, Freddie Mac, USDA, FHA and VA products. If you fully understand these loans you should understand any product your competitor is offering.

Despite the challenge of keeping current on your competitor's products, it is important that you do so. For example, if a real estate agent is comparing your adjustable rate loan with that of your competitor and your initial rate is higher, you may lose the opportunity to make the loan if you are not aware of the advantages your loan may have over that of the competitor. If your product has a lower margin or a more favorable index or lower adjustment caps, it could sway the agent and borrower toward your product. There could also be a significant difference in fees for inspections or document preparation. Maybe one product has an option to convert to a fixed rate while the other does not. Or, maybe the conversion cost is significantly different. If you don't know, then you can't compare. If one loan is a 7/1 ARM and the other is a 7/23, you need to know why the 7/23 may be a higher risk loan. If you can't compare, you can't compete because you can't prove why your product is superior. Simply knowing the attributes of your loans and the competitor's loans proves that you are the expert. Ultimate success will come when the agents aren't comparing loan products, but sending all their prospective buyers directly to you.

One of your most important jobs will be explaining to real estate agents that they do not need to make loan decisions for their buyers. In fact you don't want them to make decisions for their buyers or even to influence their decision. Real estate agents typically don't fully understand all the variables and implications of each loan type and so they shouldn't be dispensing incomplete or incorrect information to homebuyers. They often only know the loan basics and that is simply not enough for making an intelligent decision. Explain to your agents that they don't need to worry about the financing because that is your job; all they need to do is refer the client to you and you will help the client select the financing that is best for them. That is what is best for the real estate agent as well. It assures that the borrower gets the most appropriate loan product, creating a happier client who is more likely to refer new customers to the agent and to you.

In some instances, you may find that a competitor's product is actually superior to your product. If you have been unable to switch the borrower to another product offered by your firm, there are a few alternatives. Try to get that same loan through a wholesaler or broker the loan to a lender that offers the product, or simply admit that the other company has a better product and recommend that the borrower use the other lender. If you continue to insist that you have a better product, when it is obvious that you do not, you will look foolish. Besides, you have probably lost this loan anyway, so use the opportunity to lay the groundwork for the next opportunity. In this way, your credibility will be enhanced and your helpfulness affirmed. The real estate agent will then generally seek an opportunity to send another loan referral your way. Keep in mind that mortgage banking is relationship sales where every decision has to be considered in terms of you long term business association with the referral source.

In addition to knowledge of the loan programs, a working knowledge of the financial markets is also important. Although the domination of the markets by short term investment instruments has caused the markets to be very susceptible to rapid change, it is important that you understand the relationship between those markets and mortgage interest rates.

This knowledge is largely necessary so that you can intelligently discuss the markets with referral source and borrowers who will frequently seek your advice on market conditions as well as where interest rates may be headed. Your ability to comprehend and intelligently discuss the factors which influence the financial markets in general and mortgage markets in particular will go far in establishing you as a knowledgeable source of information. It is also a great topic for presentations at real estate sales meetings.

Because mortgage banking is an ever changing business, your education must never end. Be certain to read your local newspaper every day, particularly the business section and local news along with the various newspapers and magazines of the real estate and mortgage industries. There are also valuable publications available from the appraisal, mortgage insurance and title insurance organizations. If possible, read *The Wall Street Journal* every day, especially the Credit Markets page. If there is a business focused newspaper or magazine for your local market, be certain to subscribe and read it as well. If the cost of these publications is prohibitive in your early years as a mortgage loan officer, your local public library will usually have them available at no cost to you. You can also find a number of websites that provide valuable financial information.

The better informed you are, the more knowledgeable you will sound and the more confidence your referral sources and borrowers will have in you and your ability as a mortgage banker and that translates into more business for you.

Chapter 8
Building a Personal Business Plan

It can easily be said that most people want to be rich and successful, but very few actually achieve that objective. For some the problem is that they don't understand the mechanism for achieving success. For other people it is simply a case of not being willing to make the sacrifices necessary to be successful. It isn't a case of opening a door and finding success; it is a case of plotting a path that has a very high probability of leading you to your goals. There are no guarantees of course, but the more you do right, the greater your potential for success. The harder you work, the luckier you get.

Over the years an urban legend developed regarding the importance of setting goals. It was a story of the Yale University class of 1953. The legend said that a survey of graduating seniors indicated that three percent of the class had set specific written financial goals while the remaining 97% had set no written financial goals. When the surviving Yale graduates were surveyed twenty years later it was reported that the accumulated assets of the three percent that had written goals exceeded the accumulated assets of the other ninety-seven percent of graduates.

Apparently, this survey never took place. But, the reason it has been referenced so often by so many motivational speakers is because there are plenty of other studies that lend substantial validity to the value of goal setting. This particular story captures the essence of the message and lends it credibility because it referenced one of the world's most revered universities. The point is that goal setting has long been recognized as an effective tool, but the "Yale study" quantified the value by applying "statistical data."

Of course, since the story is fictitious and the data isn't real, then why should it even be mentioned? First, is to let you know that if you have heard the story elsewhere that it has no basis in fact. But it is also mentioned because business leaders have consistently achieved greater success when putting their business or personal goals in writing and using them as a blueprint for their success.

Serious researchers don't simply state that they just know something works without referencing clear, verifiable, double-blind peer-reviewed research. And yet, quantifying the effectiveness of goals has always seemed elusive because it is virtually impossible to find a focus group that started at the same place and then measure their comparative success after an extended period of time. So, the "Yale study" was apparently invented to provide such validation.

There does seem to be a very clear link between setting goals and achieving success compared with simply drifting through life without clearly defined objectives and hoping for the best. Goals give you a roadmap focused on your objectives and a timeline of your choosing. It isn't much different than company managers writing business plans that create objectives, make projections and establish benchmarks for a company. But this time it is more important because these are your goals and this is your life.

Goal setting can be a very complex process but it can also be an extremely easy process. Simply list all the things that you need to accomplish; prioritize them, list the steps necessary to reach each goal and then create a very tight time line that forces you to complete each task and meet every benchmark on your list.

Taking the time and effort to sit down and analyze your goals and to set out a clear roadmap with specific steps that are designed to help you reach each benchmark along the way will help you think through each of your objectives, including some alternatives or optional objectives. By doing this you can identify the potential obstacles and build options into the plan just in case the primary choice does not work as desired. It also helps you identify those things which you thought were important but may not actually make a contribution to the achievement of your core objectives.

Naturally, all goals are subject to periodic review and update, so don't be concerned that you are stuck with a goal forever just because you write it into your personal business plan. Your goals can be changed and should be reviewed at least once a year to determine if the goals that you previously listed are still relevant and, if so, whether you are on track to meet the benchmarks to achieve those goals. Most of all, keep in mind that you will encounter obstacles along the way. Know that they are simply obstacles, not insurmountable barriers, but merely challenges that can be overcome, circumvented or in some cases, ignored. With appropriate planning, when "Plan A" isn't successful you already have "Plan B" and "Plan C" waiting in the wings.

Advance planning that includes options saves time and gives greater clarity to the path to your goals. It also helps you determine whether Plan A really should be your first choice or whether Plan "B" or "C" may be the better option. Including options in your personal business plan is vital, because although you know where you are going and the steps to reach your objectives, the people around you don't have a copy of that script. There is nothing that tells them what they are supposed to do or when you expect them to do it. And then there is the problem that other people simply don't care about your business plan because they are focused on their own plan. So, you need to have flexibility and options when other people are too clueless to understand that they are supposed to follow your plan.

True success is the progressive realization of your goals. This means that you are successful not only when you reach the pinnacle of the mountain, but also as you are continuing to meet the benchmarks you have set along the path to your personal mountain top. An important thing to remember is that success relates only to the goals that you have set for yourself, not the goals others have set for you. Achieving someone else's goals seldom offers the degree of satisfaction that comes from achieving your own objectives. Other people's goals are for other people and are irrelevant to you.

However, if your employer's goals do not correspond with your goals, then you may be faced with making a decision regarding your continued employment with that firm. In most cases, employers set goals that are achievable by the average performer.

So, if their goals appear to be too difficult, you need to assess those goals in relation to your willingness to commit to the work and the sacrifices necessary to achieve moderate objectives.

Your success starts with identifying your goals. What do you want from life? Your goals should include far more than just your business objectives because everything in your life is interrelated. Is your objective money, travel, or perhaps achievement in a particular field such as mortgage banking or simply the freedom to do as you please? Perhaps it is providing security for you and your family, or providing you with sufficient income or resources to pursue charitable work or to return to school in order to build your skills or to seek employment in other fields which are of greater interest to you.

No matter what your eventual objectives may be, money is the master key that opens the door to virtually any world that you envision. Money can be the tool that allows you to achieve other objectives that are more important in your life than the money alone. And since the financial remuneration is the generally perceived reward of a successful mortgage loan officer, we will assume that it is your objective as well; even if you have more far-reaching goals beyond mortgage lending.

Don't be dissuaded from lofty financial goals by the old Biblical phrase referring to money being the root of all evil. That phrase is often used out of context. I sometimes feel that those who use that statement either have money and want to maintain the exclusivity of their rarefied position by discouraging others from achieving parity with them or they are people who have been unable to attain money and are trying to dilute its value to validate their own lack of success. The true Biblical phrase is "love of money is the root of all evil." This means that when your veneration of money is so great that you put its accumulation ahead of the welfare of your family and the well being of others, then it becomes a negative force in your life and the lives of others. The value of money isn't so much what it can buy for you, but the freedom it gives you. Money is simply a commodity that you trade for shelter, food, good health, safety, comfort and enjoyment for you, your family and others in your community. Use it wisely and enjoy what it brings to your life.

Before you can begin to enjoy the freedom that money can provide you must acquire an amount sufficient to pay for all the essential expenses in your life such as food, shelter, utilities and clothing. Having reached this point you can then begin to accumulate some discretionary income that you can use for savings, investments and some of the more enjoyable activities in life. Please note that savings and investments precede the enjoyable activities. If you start spending your money before you have accumulated a comfortable cushion of investment and reserve funds you will be risking your future because interest rates and the underlying housing market upon which mortgage banking depends, can be very volatile so you need to prepare yourself for the negative market fluctuations with cash reserves and minimal debt.

To determine how much money you will need to live the life you envision, you should create a budget and establish goals that are tied to the income that you will need to meet each of your objectives. Because you can never achieve a goal unless it is defined, you must first determine what your objective is. This is analogous to knowing what your target is before you fire a gun. Blindly squeezing the trigger will cause you to hit something, but it will generally be the wrong thing. But, if you have set out a target, taken time to learn how to use firearms and then you carefully aim at the target, you can measure your level of success and determine what adjustments may be required in order to hit the bulls-eye.

The first task you must undertake is to determine what goals are important to you in each area of your life. Your goals should be realistic, but challenging and progressively more substantial. You need to take the time to decide what your benchmarks should be for this year and each of the next four years, in order to have an initial five year plan. Then, take a look at where you want to be at each ten year interval and at retirement.

While some will argue that you can't possible know where you want to be in ten or twenty years, it is important to think about where you currently believe that you would like to be at each of those benchmarks. Remember, goals are easily changed if something in your life changes, but if you don't have goals and plans for your future, you will not know what steps you need to take to reach each of your goals. Without plotting the direction you want to go you may simply be right where you are now ten or twenty years from now or some other place where you may definitely not want to be.

Among the areas you should consider when setting goals are: income, assets in terms of cash, investments, property, etc., debts in terms of home mortgage, installment loans and revolving debts, including the amount of the monthly debt obligation. You should also think about other personal objectives such as marriage, family and other relationship considerations, children and education, spiritual interests, recreation, health and personal fitness. All of these things, as well as other areas of personal interest and concern that play a part in your life and which are essential to have a balanced life, need to be reviewed individually and in relation to the other objectives.

For a period of time, your income may need to increase to correspond with your increasing obligations. As you get closer to retirement, you will probably want to reduce your debts and monthly obligations so that they correspond to your post retirement income. In fact, as you have probably recognized from reviewing the financial position of your mortgage loan applicants, it is always the debt that hurts them. Acquiring a home or even an automobile that you need for work is difficult without acquiring debt to finance its purchase but you are always best served to pay off these obligations as fast as possible and be debt-free.

If you don't plan all of these things in advance, you may find that you are not sufficiently prepared for some of the major events in your life. In fact, most people find that they have insufficiently prepared for many life events. An often used expression says that if you fail to plan then you are planning to fail. Plan for your success not your failure. There are many reasons people don't achieve their goals in life but by failing to set goals and delineating the steps necessary to achieve those goals, they don't even know what benchmarks they need to reach within certain time frames to meet their objectives.

Exactly how you set out your goals is not as important as the fact that you do so. You can read books on goal setting or buy goal setting software to help you commit your goals to written form or you can consult with a financial planner or simply sit down with pencil (the eraser will come in very handy) and paper and write out what you want to achieve and the steps necessary to meet those objections. The critical point is that your goals must be in writing; writing your goals makes them real.

Many people who work through the financial goal setting exercise for the first time are astonished at how far off their actual financial situation is from where they need to be at various stages of their life. In most cases, people realize that they will need to earn far more income than they currently have, or scale down their objectives and eliminate a lot more debt. On the other hand, you may be pleasantly surprised at how well you are doing. In any event, you will find that this is one of the most important and valuable exercises you will ever undertake and it can be critical to achieving success in every aspect of your life. It lets you know where you are and what you need to do to meet your objectives. And, keep in mind, it is far better to learn about a potential shortfall now and be able to adjust your income, expenses, etc., than to find out at retirement that you grossly misjudged your financial plan and that you are far short of the funds you need to retire or that you may never be able to afford to retire.

Chapter 9
Evaluate Your Loan Volume Requirements

There is an easy formula to determine how your goals and objectives relate to the number of loans you need to produce each year to reach the income level that you seek. It is important to make this assessment before identifying your potential referral sources, because it tells you how many loans you will need to generate and it gives you a general idea of how many referral sources you may need. Since most people have a greater sense of annual earnings than of loan volume, you should choose an income that you would like to earn in the next twelve months. Be realistic. If you have been earning $40,000 per year as a loan officer, don't immediately set your goal at $300,000, although you can easily reach earnings of that level or greater. But it is a process that may take two or three years to reach 80% of your potential and up to five years to hit your maximum production level.

There are loan officers who have personal incomes well in excess of a million dollars per year and you can too, but it takes judicious planning and hard work. Keep in mind that the objective of this book is to help you make dramatic gains in your income, but those gains will only come when you have so ingrained these marketing techniques and highly productive work habits so that they are second nature to you. From that point forward you can expect your income to jump exponentially for several years until you reach your personal production capacity. At that point you can leverage your time and ability to produce even more business and generate an even higher income by hiring one or more assistants.

To assess the dollar volume and number of loans that you need to produce in order to earn the income you desire, use the formulas in the following two charts. The calculations will tell you how much activity you will need to generate in order to achieve your objectives. Because there are so many variables, your results will certainly vary, but it will get you aimed in the right direction. From there, you can make adjustments to more accurately reflect what you want to achieve in relation to what is happening in your market. Also recognize that referral sources take time to cultivate but with appropriate attention, the results will materialize.

You may want to put the following formula into a spread sheet like Excel so that you can change various factors. For example, your compensation rate may change with higher loan production; or you may close more or less than 80% of your applications (line 6 of Chart 1), so you will want to make those and any other adjustment to reflect your specific situation. *The factors in the formulas have been included simply to provide examples and serve as guidance.*

CHART 1

Formula for converting target income into activities:

1.	Annual Income Target (insert your personal income goal)	$300,000
2.	Average Loan Amount (insert the average loan in your area)	$275,000
3.	Compensation Rate (insert your personal compensation rate)	.50%
4.	Income Per-Closed Loan (multiply line 2 by line 3)	$1,375
5.	Closed Loans Needed to Meet Annual Goal (divide line 1 by line 4)	218
6.	Percentage of Your Applications that Close and Fund	80%
7.	Number of Annual Applications Needed (divide line 5 by line 6)	273
8.	Percentage of Borrower Interviews that Result in Applications	60%
9.	Number of Borrower Interviews Needed (divide line 7 by line 8)	455
10.	Number of Business Days Per-Year (5 days per week x 48 weeks [4 week's vacation])	240
11.	Number of Borrower Interviews Needed Per-Day (divide line 9 by line 10)	1.89
12.	Percentage of Inquiry Calls that Result in Interviews	40%
13.	Number of Daily Inquiry Calls Needed (divide line 11 by line 12)	4.73
14.	Number of Monthly Inquiry Calls Required (multiply line 13 by 20 business days)	**94.70**

Now that you know how many inquiry calls you need from your referral sources each month (line 14 of Chart 1), you need to figure out how many referral sources it will take to generate that number of calls. To determine that number, divide the result of line 14 of Chart 1 by line 5 of Chart 2. The actual results will depend on how many referral sources you have, the type of sources, and of course the number of referrals that you can expect each month from each source.

CHART 2

This second chart is very speculative as it has many variables. However, it is included here because it helps keep referral sources and related business in perspective and provides a sense of the number of referral sources you may need to generate the level of income you wish to achieve. The only guarantee is that your actual experience will not match these projected amounts but you still need to reproduce this chart using the number of referral sources that send business to you in order to weigh it against the number of monthly inquiry calls that you need to achieve your annual income target (line 14 of Chart 1).

	Type of Referral Source	Number of Referral Sources	Monthly Referrals from Each Source	Total Monthly Referrals
1.	Primary Real Estate Agents (top 10% of agents)	10	5.00	50
2.	Secondary Real Estate Agents (next 20% of agents)	20	2.50	50
3.	Tertiary Real Estate Agents (remaining 70% of agents)	30	.50	15
4.	General Referral Sources (other than real estate agents)	60	.25	15
5.	Total Referral Sources and Referrals	120		**130**

While these numbers are generally representative, they are extrapolated from a lot of data with a very wide range of results, so your results will probably be substantially different. Keep in mind that Line 5, Column 3 of Chart 2 represents the total referrals from all your referral sources *if* they provide the estimated number of monthly referrals and *if* you have the number of referral sources in Column 1 of Chart 2. The bottom line is that if Line 5, Column 3 of Chart 2 exceeds the number in Line 14 of Chart 1 then you should meet your production and income goals.

Keep in mind that if you have a proportionally higher number of real estate agents that you consider to be primary agents (top 10% of agents), the total number of sources that you may need could be lower as each source will be worth more referral calls to you. To some degree, this first data point will be determined by which agents you classify as primary, secondary and tertiary as well as how many you have in each category. Of course, there is also the question of what percentage of their referrals each agent sends to you rather than some other far less deserving loan officer.

One of the obvious questions you may ask is that given the declining rate of referrals when comparing primary agents with the other sources, why even bother with referral sources that are not primary in nature? The answer is that the level of referrals will change from each source over time and some secondary and tertiary real estate agents will grow to be primary. If you aren't their mortgage source when they start out at the bottom, you are less likely to become their lending source later. There is also the difficulty of immediately developing meaningful business relationships with those real estate agents whom you identify as "primary" level agents. They probably got to be primary agents by building their business over a period of time which means that they probably have established relationships with other mortgage bankers as well as a long list of loan officers who are courting them. With enough effort you can become their primary mortgage banker, but it may not happen overnight. The bottom line is that this entire process generally falls into the category of not having all your eggs in one basket. Diversify your marketing efforts to cultivate a cross-section of agents. Over time you will probably trim your list of agents, moving some from one category to another and some will be totally eliminated from your agent list. This way you will always be focusing on the agents that are sending a significant amount of business to you, while keeping a "farm team" in the wings.

If you pro-rate the amount of your personal time and marketing dollars spent on each source in proportion to the amount of client referrals that you receive from them, then you will be getting the same return on your time and dollar investment with every referral source. It may take a while to recognize the volume that you can expect from each source and to adjust your commitment of time and marketing dollars invested in each source. Here is an example of how to distribute your time and marketing dollars if you have five referral sources:

Chart 3.

Referral Source Number	Number of referrals from each source	Percentage of referrals received from each source
1	5	14%
2	9	26%
3	2	6%
4	12	34%
5	7	20%
TOTAL	**35**	**100%**

Based on Chart 3, you should invest 6% of your time and marketing dollars on referral source number 3 and 26% on source number 2, etc.

When calculating referrals for Chart 1, inquiry calls have been separated from interviews and applications simply because very active agents will refer every prospect to you to be pre-approved for financing so that they know that the borrower is qualified to buy and has their financing ready to complete the purchase. Many of these prospects may really not be ready to buy and others may not currently qualify for available financing so they are categorized as "inquiries." However, it benefits you to talk with them because it gives you the opportunity to develop a relationship with the prospect so that when they are ready to buy or refinance, you are the loan officer to whom they turn. It also gives you a wonderful opportunity to follow-up with the referral source after you have spoken with the prospective buyer/borrower to tell the referral source the result of your conversation. When the "inquiry" call identifies a valid prospect, those calls transition into "interview" calls where you begin to refine the type of financing that may be appropriate for the prospective applicant while you concurrently sell them on choosing you as their mortgage banker. When the "interview" process has been successful, the potential borrower transitions again into the position where they submit an application for financing.

Chapter 10
Exemplary Client Service

There are few things that you can do as a mortgage banker that will ingratiate you to your clients and your referral sources more than being highly responsive to their calls, emails and other inquiries. It is crucial that you answer your phone every time you can during your business hours because referral sources, particularly real estate agents, will call the next loan officer on their list when you don't answer.

Although you will need to commit twelve or more hours of hard work each day to build your mortgage banking practice, that doesn't mean that you should make yourself available to clients and referral sources all hours of the day and night. There is such a thing as being too available. It makes you look desperate for business and unprofessional. Virtually all professionals, be they lawyers, accountants, physicians or mortgage bankers typically have scheduled business hours.

Balancing your availability helps you develop your image as a professional. For example, you could specify your business hours as 10 AM to 8 PM when you are available to take calls and meet with prospective borrowers. Outside of those hours, people may leave a voice mail message which you may return during your business hours. Naturally you can return calls outside of those hours but when you do so, you set a precedent that referral sources and real estate agents in particular, will always expect a return call.

There is an old saying that there are two rules regarding customer service. The first rule is that "The customer is always right." The second rule is "When you think the customer is wrong, refer to rule number one." In other words, no matter how impertinent a customer may be, simply step back, take a deep breath, smile and tell them that you are delighted to assist them. However, never continue a business relationship with a borrower or referral source that is abusive.

When a prospective borrower has been referred to you it is very important that you call the referral source IMMEDIATELY (within an hour or LESS) after talking with the prospective borrower. This quick response lets your referral sources know that you are taking care of the people that they refer to you, regardless of whether they are currently a candidate for financing. When they are not an immediate candidate, you can offer the referral source, particularly if it is a real estate agent, some guidance as to how to work with this candidate to bring them along as a buyer for the future. It helps build that bond with the agents so that they continue to rely on you and refer other prospective borrowers.

A large part of your job is to constantly remind every referral source to always provide you with the name and phone number of every viable prospect they talk with so that you can get them pre-approved for financing. It puts each prospect that much closer to buying a home and the real estate agent that much closer to collecting their brokerage fee.

It is important that your referral sources tell their prospects that you will call them. Naturally, you then need to call them

IMMEDIATELY (within an hour or LESS). Don't wait for the prospective borrower to call you because they will probably get distracted and ultimately end up talking with some other loan officer. You work hard to build referral sources; don't let the fruit of your labor wilt on the vine by failing to follow up on every single potential business source. Besides, you need to talk with the prospective borrower before you can report on your conversation to the source that referred them to you. If you are unable to reach the prospective borrower when you call, give the referral source a quick call to let them know that and assure them that you will let them know as soon as you talk with the prospect. Good communication with your referral sources is essential to maintaining a good business relationship with them.

The time involved in handling each of the inquiry calls is substantial, but they are part of the "little things" that build your business. Your marketing plan is designed to generate referrals. If you don't give them exceptional service then your efforts have been wasted. From the point where you make contact with the potential borrower it is up to your product knowledge, sales skills and ability to "connect" with the prospect that will determine your level of success. While most of us hate to "role play," you may find it highly beneficial to rehearse phone calls and in-person sales calls with other loan officers before you begin calling prospective referral sources and talking with borrowers.

It is essential that you have a website where prospective borrowers can complete a pre-approval request as well as a full mortgage loan application. Since not all prospects are comfortable with computer technology or providing personal information through the Internet, you will also need a paper application package prepared in advance that you can send to clients by e-mail, fax, FedEx or USPS. Your ability to accommodate everyone by providing an application option that is within their comfort zone will greatly increase your loan volume.

By having the borrowers complete the mortgage application on your website, or completing a paper application that can be sent to them and then returned to you, a lot of time is saved. In some cases it will be necessary for you to meet with the prospective borrower in person to complete the loan application and that significantly impairs your efficiency. However, it is better than not getting the loan application at all. When possible, have your processor or assistant take care of the in-person applications. Your job is to obtain the referrals that bring the customer in the door. You are the rainmaker and the public relations arm of your mortgage banking practice. The more you can delegate the perfunctory activities to other people, the more time you will have for business development and the more efficient and productive you will become.

Chapter 11
Defining Your Territory

What is your "territory?" There are probably as many descriptions of "territory" as there are mortgage companies. Some companies adhere to a strict territory system that is governed by geography or by a list of accounts spread throughout the region. Other lenders consider a real estate office to be a protected account; others focus on individual agents. Many companies follow an open system where having more than one loan officer calling on the same real estate office is just fine. If you get the business then the real estate agent is your account and if another loan officer gets the business then the agent is their account; at least until the next referral.

If you have a choice in how your territory is defined, start with a small geographic area so that you can efficiently visit your clients, including real estate agents, professional referral sources and retail merchants as well as your prospective clients. Try to use Zip Code territories because that will make it easier to extract names of real estate agents and other licensed professionals from state licensing board databases for marketing purposes.

Even if your company allows other loan officers from your office to call on the same real estate office, you are best served if you have a compact area in which your referral sources are concentrated. If you have to waste time and gasoline driving all over town, you will have less time for productive business development. Ultimately you will make most of your sales calls by telephone but initially and periodically thereafter it is crucial that referral sources regularly see your smiling face. Put a lot of emphasis on "smiling."

Because mortgage banking is relationship driven, periodic personal face-to-face visits are critical to your success. Choosing the number of referral sources, both real estate and others tends to be a decision that is often governed by the rules of your company. There are successful loan officers with as few as five real estate brokerage offices and as many as one hundred. Of course one hundred offices from which no business emanates are of no value. Start with 5 to 10 offices and perfect your marketing skills. As business develops, add more offices and agents. The same is true of professional referral sources and retail merchants. The focus should be on the productivity of the referral sources rather than their number. It is counter-productive to market to a large number of unproductive sources.

When choosing a geographic area, consider that most of your loans will be on properties in or near that area so the higher priced the homes, the larger the mortgages and with most loan officers compensation being based on the loan amount, the more money you are likely to make on each transaction. However, the borrowers on higher value properties are generally more knowledgeable, better educated and more informed consumers who shop price more aggressively partly because a difference of .125% in rate translates into a much larger dollar difference in their monthly payment than it would on a smaller mortgage ($16 per month on a $200,000 loan vs. $81 per month on a $1,000,000 loan. You may therefore have to shave something off the rate so that you will make less on each loan, but a greater volume of high dollar loans can put much more money in your pocket.

In areas of lower value homes, FHA and VA financing are more prevalent due to the low down-payment requirement and more flexible credit standards. The potential benefit is that some lenders pay higher commissions on government loans because they generally have more value in the secondary market. Government loans often require more work and, for this reason, the lower price market may be underserved by lenders, making it easier for you to create a level of dominance due to less competition.

Areas where homes are of "average" value for the region generally have more consistent turn-over and borrowers with fewer income and credit issues compared with government lending areas. However, this is the market that most loan officers inhabit so the competition may be particularly fierce.

Virtually every successful, high income mortgage loan officer works in high value areas. Of course there are a lot of unsuccessful loan officers working in those areas as well but that is true in every area. Most loan officers have a blend of markets but they tend to be weighted toward one economic stratum. If your territory is close to your office then that is good because it makes the real estate agents easily accessible to you and it makes your office easily accessible to them and their clients. Part of your business development effort is to make everything as easy as possible for referral sources and prospective clients to conduct business with you.

If you are new to the mortgage business you may be more comfortable working with agents and borrowers who are less challenging until you have more experience, knowledge and confidence in your ability to work with borrowers with complex income and tax structures. You can always transition your mortgage banking practice toward the higher value properties and the agents who dwell in that environment. Or, you may find a niche in a more modest market where you become the acknowledged expert and where you meet your personal income goals through more loans rather than fewer transactions with higher loan amounts. Ultimately, you will probably need to include high end clients if you plan to earn a high six figure to seven figure income.

Depending on the community where you work, your choices may be limited. Look at your company's compensation plan and product offering before making a decision. If, for example, your company has a higher compensation rate for government loans make a quick calculation to compare what you will earn with a typical government loan versus a typical conventional loan. Also consider what you may be paid on a jumbo loan. In these calculations, assume that you will have to absorb a small rate reduction and therefore a reduced commission on most jumbo loans and that you may be able to earn some overage on some of the conventional and government loans. Regardless of the prevalent financing in your market area, you will still need to be an expert or at least very competent, on all financing types.

Chapter 12
Where is the Business?

Business is literally everywhere. But not everyone is actively looking for a mortgage loan today. Therefore, your marketing plan needs to have a long term focus encompassing prospective individual borrowers as well as referral sources that represent a more efficient means of generating business because they can direct a regular stream of customers to you. Each individual referral source will have quirks that you must recognize and accommodate, so invest in lots of Chap Stick® because you will need to do a lot of "kissing-up."

While there will be more explicit information on these sources later, here are some of the businesses that are likely to refer a substantial number of prospective mortgage clients.

Business comes from many sources including the following:

- Real estate industry
  - ° Real estate agents
  - ° Builders
  - ° Land developers
  - ° Home renovation contractors
  - ° Architects
  - ° Civil engineers
  - ° Association memberships (Realtors®, builders, etc.)

- Professional practitioners
  - ° Financial planners
  - ° Accountants
  - ° Certified Public Accountants
  - ° Attorneys
  - ° Insurance Agents
  - ° Association memberships Bar Association, Financial Planners, etc.

- Direct relationship referrals
  - ° Personal friends as well as friends and colleagues of your spouse or life partner
  - ° Civic club members Health club / gym members

- Community organizations
  - ° PTA affiliations
  - ° Parents of your children's friends
  - ° Neighbors
  - ° Personal business contacts such as your dry cleaner, auto mechanic, hair stylist, personal physician, pharmacist, lawyer, accountant, dentist, etc.

- Retail merchants
  - Auto sales representatives
  - Motor home and travel trailer dealers
  - Furniture stores
  - Billiard and pool table retailers
  - Paving contractors
  - Swimming pool contractors
  - Heating and air conditioning contractors
  - Boat dealers
- Other business sources
  - Farm a residential community
  - Homebuyer seminars
  - Relocation companies
  - Corporate human resource departments
  - Small banks' construction lending department
  - Credit unions that don't offer mortgage lending
  - Stock brokers
  - Physicians
  - Business owners
  - Membership in the Chamber of Commerce, merchants associations, etc.
  - Direct advertising

Now that you know who you may be targeting to obtain referral business, you need to do your research to get names and build a comprehensive database, so that you not only know who your contacts are, but you know a lot of relevant information about them. That personal knowledge of individual referral sources is something you will acquire over time, primarily from conversations with the individuals, but it is essential for developing close, permanent, productive business relationships. It's those relationships that are essential to generating client referrals and mortgage applications. Oh yes, and for making money.

Chapter 13
Building a Database

Now the real work begins. You need to build a comprehensive database of all your referral sources. This will take a lot of time and a lot of work. However, once the database is set up you will only need an hour or so each evening to update the database with the information you have gathered during that day. Be certain to complete your updates daily or the backlog will become daunting.

The format for your database is strictly up to you. Microsoft Access is probably the most appropriate software because you can structure it exactly as you like. It can be purchased individually or as part of the Microsoft Office Professional package. ACT contact management software is useful as well. Several large lenders provide ACT to their loan officers which they specifically tailor for the lender's purposes. It has the benefit of uploading all the borrower information from your loan applications directly to their server so that you can track your borrowers and other referral sources and produce follow-up letters. Of course, if you ever leave that employer, you can't copy your data and take it with you because their customization will probably make it incompatible with ACT software that you buy off the shelf, and the uploaded data usually cannot be retrieved. Therefore, if you work for a lender that uses proprietary or customized commercial software, you should also input the relevant information into your personal database.

If you prefer a more robust database program you can purchase Oracle CRM, IBM DB2 or Microsoft CRM. However, you can also use Microsoft Excel if you are looking for a relatively simple database. All the database programs allow you to produce mail merge letters and generate lists of your various referral sources. The question is whether you are willing to put in a lot of time to become a database expert or whether you want to focus on being a successful mortgage banker. It doesn't hurt to be both, but your time is extremely valuable so I suggest using a program like Access or ACT because they are simple to set up and easy to use.

When developing your database, segregate your referral sources into separate database categories either by using the categories listed in Chapter 12 or any other method that suits you. Each group of referral sources and clients require similar information with only a few differences. You can create one standard database format for businesses and another one for individuals. Although you will not use all the data fields for every referral source it is much easier to have only one template for businesses and one template for individuals. Keep in mind that you are the one who has to use this system, so make it easy for you.

Consider setting up separate folders and sub-folders for each business type, such as real estate brokers, with a subset for each real estate company and an additional subset for each agent at the respective real estate firms.

When you set up your database templates, input the information from a few representative sources just to see if it does everything that you want it to do. If you need to add more data fields it is easier to do it when you have only a few sources listed. Here is an example of how to set up data fields:

For client databases, you need to include the names of the borrower and co-borrower but place each name in a separate field. Consider using field identifiers that are preceded with a "B" for the borrower and "C" for co-borrower. Here is an example of field identifiers: "BPrefix" (Mr., Ms., Dr. etc.) "BFirstName" (Robert), "BMNI" (J.), "BLastName" (Smith), "BSuffix" (Jr.), "BNickName" (Bob). Then do the same for the co-borrower using the following: "CPrefix" (Mr., Ms., Dr. etc.) "CFirstName" (Susan), "CMNI" (L.), "CLastName" (Smith), "CSuffix" ( ), "CNickName" (Sue). The field "MNI" is an abbreviation for "Middle Name or Initial." For referral sources, use the same format but use an "R" for "referral" as the first letter in each field identifier, such as "RPrefix," etc.

Follow the same format for other items such as addresses. Consider using the following format: "Number" (1600), "Street" (Pennsylvania Avenue, N.W.), "City" (Washington), "State" (DC), "Zip" (20500). It never hurts to separate data into its component parts because it can be very painful to divide fields later.

The advantage of dividing the categories in this manner is that you can send a mail merged letter or note where the envelope is addressed as "Mr. & Ms. Robert J. Smith, Jr." and the letter inside can have a salutation of "Dear Bob & Sue." Keep in mind that during the application and processing period and up through closing your formal communications with the borrowers should always address them as "Robert J. Smith, Jr. and Susan L. Smith." In conversations and with personal notes during processing you can address them as Bob and Sue and certainly, you can be less formal in your correspondence after the closing. It is worth taking the time to make your database flexible with extra fields when you set it up as it is an arduous task to do it later.

If you are sending letters to all your current or former clients and you haven't put the extra fields in your database you may be stuck with using their more formal given names rather than their nick names. You may also be forced to including the prefix and suffix if you put the borrower's full name all in one field. This will most certainly make your correspondence seem rather stilted and formal when you want each of your borrowers to think of you not only as their mortgage banker but also as their friend.

Include the street address of your borrower's current residence and their new address if they buy and finance a new home. You might even leave room for a third, fourth or fifth address as many of your clients will remain with you for your entire career and buy new homes and refinance many times.

Be certain to include the client's home phone number, cell phone number, home fax, business phone, and business fax as well as their personal email address. Include fields for each borrower's employer, their title plus space for additional employers as they grow in their career. Always leave a field for miscellaneous notes.

When you are inputting telephone numbers, be certain to use all ten digits of the phone number. Due to growth in the number of phones, many regions are adding more Area Codes with some areas splitting territories into two or more Area Codes and other areas using overlay Area Codes where you could have two phones in the same household with different Area Codes. People can now move from one area of the country to another and keep the same Area Code with their cell phone. The Area Code as we have known it as a geographically defined number is disappearing.

Include fields for the names of your client's children, with fields for their first and last names including year of birth. If you use the child's age instead of year of birth you will need to update the pages every year. Otherwise, ten years later you may think that their 14 year old is still only 4 years old. If you know the name of their school and the activities in which they participate such as sports, music, etc. that is useful as well. Always be very careful when asking about your client's children and their activities. There is a very fine line between being a friend who is interested in the family and their children and being viewed as taking an inappropriate interest. However, most people are happy to talk about their family and will volunteer the information without you having to ask for it, especially if you offer a little information about your family first.

For business referrals, include the business name, address and phone numbers. Leave space for the names of staff members with whom you may interact. And be certain to leave that extra field for miscellaneous notes.

For individual referral sources such as real estate agents you should include space for the person's photo. Many agents put their picture in ads as well as on brochures, business cards and of course their website. You can copy or scan the photo into your database from any of these sources and that could be invaluable in helping you remember each agent. You may need to scan the photo into your "pictures" folder and then open the database page and click on the "insert" tab. Select the "picture" icon then chose the correct agent's photo from the "pictures" folder. Click the "insert" tab and the photo should be copied into your database. Just keep in mind that each computer operating system and software may be slightly different.

Before you invest too much time inputting data, be certain you have a system for backing up your database as well as everything else on your computer. If you have a system crash, or your computer picks up a virus, worm or other malevolent program, your entire business could be in jeopardy. You can use a program like Crash Plan at www.crashplan.com, which offers free software to backup your computer to another computer that you may have or that of a friend. Don't be concerned that your friend can see your data as it appears as gibberish when viewed by them. For a charge you can backup to Crash Plan's computer. Another source is www.mozy.com where you can backup to their servers for around five dollars per month. It is beneficial to have a data backup repository that is "off-site." That way, if you have a fire or your home is impacted by any other disaster, your data will be safely stored at another location.

To build your database you need to identify as many individuals as possible in each category. In many cases you can simply call the agency in your state government that regulates each profession licensed in your state and request a list of the licensed individuals. This is public information and should be readily available to you although you may be charged a fee to cover their cost of providing the information to you.

Most data from the state will be provided on a CD or e-mailed to you. Before you begin to manipulate the data, make a working copy of the information from the state and store the original in a special folder on your computer for original databases. By keeping all the original databases in a separate folder you can go back and copy all or part of them if you need to do so, but never change the original although you can probably go back to the state agency and get another copy if you need to do so. Next, apply the "sort" function on your working copy to sort the data by Zip Code. Copy the information from the database for the specific Zip Codes where you intend to market your mortgage banking services and put it in a new database or simply delete the information for the Zip Codes where you do not intend to market. Keep in mind that you can always go back to your original database to obtain information that you may have deleted.

You should periodically request updated lists from the state agencies so that you have the names of people who are newly licensed as well as identifying those who are no longer licensed. When you do this, start with your "territory database" using only the Zip Codes where you are marketing your services. Then highlight the entire database and change the font color of the data to "red" for example. Then sort and copy the data from the Zip Codes that you use from the new database from the state and place it in your working copy database and make it another color such as "green." Merge the "red" data and the "green" data into one working database. Then use the "sort" tool on your computer again, sorting this time by "name." This will place duplicate information for the same individual adjacent to each other, one "red" and one "green" so that it is easy to see which information you already have. The newly licensed individuals will be in "green" without a corresponding "red" copy. Add the new "green" licensees to your database. By using the "name" sort you may see new home address for some of your existing contacts. Be sure to update your database with their new address. Of course if your referral sources are the loyal individuals that we all know that they are, you should already have their new address from providing the mortgage financing for their new home.

Now, look for the few "red" names that don't have a current "green" entry. These people may have left the business, moved to another area, lost their license or even died. You may want to remove these individuals from your database. If they get licensed again, they will show up on a subsequent update from the state. Some may still be working in your area but moved to a new home in another Zip Code.

Once you have the mail lists you will need to match the individuals with their workplace. With real estate agents for example you can get a list of agents who are members of the local Realtor® Association or the multiple listing services. These lists will generally identify the real estate firm with which they are associated. You may need to join these organizations to be eligible to get the membership list, so you need to weigh the cost of that membership with the value you expect to receive. Some Realtor® Associations have their membership roster on their website. Another, less expensive, and also less effective, method is to read the real estate magazines with properties that are listed for sale and the classified newspaper ads. In these advertisements you will find the names and often the photo of some of the agents along with their real estate firm and much of their contact information, such as cell phone, email address, etc. Unfortunately, this will allow you to get information on only a limited number of agents.

In some states the names of all real estate agents licensed in each office must be made available from the office where they are associated to anyone who requests the list. If this is the case in your state, you can get the list when you meet with that office's managing broker.

A valuable benefit of obtaining the list of licensed real estate brokers and agents from the state is that it has the home address of most agents. In an age where many agents work from home, this gives you the means to reach those agents who rarely go into their real estate office.

A very good resource for the business name, address and phone number of virtually every professional business including those associated with the real estate industry is the local Yellow Pages of the phone directory. Community newspapers and regional magazines also let you know who is actively advertising and might be a good prospect for you.

Once you have the names of all the agents in a real estate office you need to update your database so that you know who is in that office. This also applies to every other referral source. However, don't wait until you have a complete database before you start making sales calls. Work with the information you have and continue to build your database and your referral source relationships along the way.

It may seem unnecessary to develop and maintain such an elaborate database since you will often be sending handwritten notes and not availing yourself of the efficiency of the mail merge option that a database offers. However, the database will have everyone's address that you will need even for the handwritten notes. There will be plenty of opportunity for you to utilize the database to send letters, postcards, flyers and other communications. Besides, you can print addresses on envelopes without offending anyone and the post office delivery person will actually be able to read it and deliver it to the right person.

At least once every quarter, consider printing out your database with a separate page for each referral source along with the separate page of notes that you have accumulated. These pages can be compiled in a notebook and kept by your phone when you are in the office or taken along in your car when you are making sales calls.

When making drop-in sales calls, before you go into the office, you can glance at the pages for the individuals in that office just to refresh your memory so that you can recall the names of as many people as possible. You may prefer just to take your laptop computer along and look up the information in your database rather than having a printed page. My experience has been that the printed notebook is easier, but you should use the method that works best for you.

If you do use a notebook, be certain to put it in the trunk of your car when you are taking an agent to lunch. You certainly don't want them picking up your notebook and looking at your confidential information, especially the less than complimentary words and phrases that you may use to help identify and remember your referral sources. Keep in mind that you may have from several hundred to a couple thousand individuals that you are working with and remembering everyone can be a huge challenge. Making a couple notes on each referral source's page in your book to relate their name with their face can be important. If they remind you of a Bull Dog and you can associate that with their name then it may help to put that term on their page just to jog your memory but you don't want any agent to see that. If they see it on one agent's page they will quickly look to see what you have written on their page.

Accumulating the information to build a database to produce a "profile sheets" for each referral source can be a major undertaking in the beginning, but it will simplify after you have gathered most of the basic information. Thereafter you will simply make a couple entries with each visit.

Initially, there will be a lot of unknown information for each real estate agent, but you can fill in the blanks as you get to know the agents and they share personal information with you. Of course, most agents now have websites so you can gather a great deal of information there.

The value of the information is immeasurable. Take the time to learn who the agents are, the names and professions of their spouses and the names, ages, schools and other activities of their children. If you do, you are well on your way to success. If you can walk into an office, say hello to an agent by name, and ask how their son Jason is doing in baseball or their daughter Kate is doing in gymnastics, you are going to be at the top of their list of mortgage bankers. There is nothing that endears you to a person more than taking an interest in their family.

Pay attention to the agent's hobbies and outside interest. Read the newspaper and look for the things that would interest your agents. Make notes on what you read and comment on these activities when you see the agent. If it is appropriate, clip out the article and mail it to them. You may be surprised by how effective personal gestures can be, and they pay big dividends.

Chapter 14
The Comprehensive Marketing Plan

To a mortgage banker, marketing is generally thought of in terms related to the secondary mortgage market. Certainly secondary marketing is one of the most critical functions of a mortgage banking firm, but primary loan officer marketing is equally important though often neglected. Primary marketing promotes the company, its sales agents (loan officers), its products and its services. The effectiveness of that marketing can make the crucial difference between mediocrity and phenomenal success. Unless prospective customers know who you are and what you have to offer, it is unlikely that they will direct business to you.

Simply having knowledge of your existence is a start, but it is not nearly enough. There must also be a favorable connotation associated with you. Marketing is the proactive process of making others aware of you and your company on terms that are most favorable to you. And since your competition will probably not make an effort to do that for you, the door is wide open for you to set the stage so that your customers and competitors alike see you in exactly the context you want to be viewed.

A significant challenge for mortgage bankers is the need to market their services to third party intermediaries such as real estate agents and other referral sources. It requires a greater level of sales skill than selling directly to the prospective customer and a significant amount of finesse. The loan officer must create a positive image and relationship with the referral source and a level of confidence that encourages the referral source to refer prospective borrowers to the loan officer. Then there must be a second sale of the loan officer's knowledge, skill and compassion for the borrower. For these reasons, it is essential that the loan officer develop a marketing program that has a focus on both the referral sources and the consumer.

One of the most important pieces of written material that you should produce to promote your mortgage banking services is an introductory brochure that you might entitle "Introducing Your Mortgage Banker." To develop content for the brochure, write a brief article about yourself from the third person perspective. The focus of the article should be your experience as a mortgage banker; especially any achievements or recognition you may have received from the mortgage banking, real estate, home building or related industries. The emphasis should be on your competence, commitment to service and product knowledge not on your production volume unless you can tie that directly to your exemplary client service.

If you are relatively new to mortgage banking, you might use some other achievement outside the industry as "filler" to give the article some "body" until you acquire more substantive mortgage experience. Be careful not to use too many superlatives in describing yourself. They will detract from the substance of the article. If you have lived in the area for a long time, be certain to mention that. If you just moved to the area, definitely do not disclose that information. Particularly in smaller communities local people receive preference over outsiders. Do mention if you attended a local college or one of your state universities or another notable educational institution.

If you were a member of a sports team or engaged in some other significant activity or received academic honors, be certain to tell your audience about that. Include the honors in a very matter-of-fact way without bragging. You can also mention your spouse, particularly if they grew up in the community or if they hold a laudable position in business or as a community volunteer. You never know, someone may recognize their name or know their family. Those things open doors for you. Never mention your pets or hobbies unless there is particular relevance. If for example you raise horses and you work in an equestrian community, then that is relevant information. People don't need to know about your Iguana named Iggy.

When you are finished writing your article, read it very carefully. If you had never met the subject of the article, what would your opinion be of the person in the article? Would you be favorably inclined to conduct business with this person based upon their qualifications and experience or would your response be neutral or negative? It is important that there be an appropriate balance of educational achievement, professional expertise and civic involvement.

Naturally, if the article projects a negative image, some drastic changes must be made. If the reaction is neutral, what can you add that will give the article a more positive impact? Even if the article presents a favorable impression, is there anything else that can be added or deleted that will enhance its impact? After you have finished your editing, ask a confidant to review the article and to offer constructive suggestions.

After you are satisfied with your article, take the essence of that information and craft it into the text of your "Introducing Your Mortgage Banker" brochure. The brochure needs to be professional, tasteful and present you in a very positive manner. Be absolutely certain that the text is presented from the third person perspective. If you ever use "I" in the text then it is wrong. The objective of this brochure is to give you credibility, while providing you with something that you can mail or personally deliver to your prospective referral sources. By using the third person perspective, it will sound as though someone else is bragging about you rather than you telling people what a wonderful person and exceptional mortgage banker you are.

The ultimate format of your brochure is up to you but you might consider preparing it on the computer using an 8 ½" x 11" page in landscape layout with two columns. When folded it becomes an 8 ½" x 5 ½" brochure. This size can fit into a standard 5 ¾" x 8 ¾" greeting card envelope. Of course you can also produce a three column brochure from the same size paper with two folds that easily fits into a #10 envelope. A heavy card stock makes for a nice brochure and you can print these brochures directly from your home computer. Folding heavy card stock is challenging unless you purchase, rent or borrow a folding machine and even then the heavy card stock can be problematic. However, lighter weight stock isn't as striking.

You can print brochures using a color laser printer or have them printed by a commercial printing company. In the long run it may be cheaper to have the brochures of any size produced by a printing company after you have developed the style and text. You could also have a professional marketing firm or printer with a creative shop produce the brochure for you.

Printing your brochures from your computer allows you to print as few or as many as you need and then make changes as often as you choose. It is a bit of a compromise compared with having a couple thousand brochures printed and ready to use, but it also gives you the flexibility to tweak the content before committing to print a large number of brochures and then determining that something could be written better. On the other hand you can waste too much time trying to make everything perfect. That is called "perfection procrastination" where you spend so much time trying to make something so perfect that you never actually get the job done. When you are satisfied with the format and text, have a commercial printer print at least a thousand brochures.

Consider having several variations of your brochure. Create one brochure for real estate agents and a second one for other referral sources emphasizing the value of entrusting their clients to your high quality care. A third brochure could be focused on prospective first time homebuyers that can be distributed to rental apartments. A fourth version can be distributed to condominiums and single family homes for the purchase of another home or the refinance of their present property. Most of the information will be the same with just a slight adjustment for each audience. The important part is that the contact information is yours, not the company's.

If you decide to print your own brochures, be certain that the right and left borders are one-half the center space(s). That will give the brochure a balanced look when it is folded. When preparing the brochure on your computer, the column on the left of the first sheet will become the back cover of the brochure and the column on the right will become the front cover.

The second page will be the two or three inside columns for your text. If you use three columns for example, the first column on the left can contain the condensed the article about you. In the center you can provide some information about your company and a brief description of a few particularly appealing or unusual loan products that you offer. The column on the right side could contain your photo with your phone number and email address. If you have the ability for prospective borrowers to complete a loan application online then include your web address. The inclusion of this information limits the amount of self aggrandizement that you need to fill space. Remember, the format and content are entirely up to you.

Your next task is to have your photograph taken by a professional photographer. No, you can't use that photo with you and your friends at the bar or the one from the post office wall with that very special number under your photo. Usually photographers can provide you with TIF or JPEG files that you can put on your computer for multiple uses. You might also want a copy with a PHG tag that can be used directly in your web site. Copy your photograph to the front of the brochure under the words "Introducing Your Mortgage Banker" and above your name and the name of your company. Add a second copy of the photo to the right panel inside the brochure. The pose in the photo should be business like, but not somber; a smile is good. Use only one pose for all your marketing material because that makes it easy for people to identify your name with your face. Be certain that you are professionally dressed for the photo.

The purpose of this marketing piece is to get your name and face in front of every real estate sales agent, builder and other referral source in your territory. It gives you an opportunity to tell about your experience in a way that would be awkward if done in person. It also removes the need for you to explain your experience, talent, knowledge, etc. This marketing piece gives you the opportunity to tell everyone exactly what you want them to know about you in the way you want it said. When you give a brochure to a referral source, simply say, "this will tell you a little about me; it is important that you know something about people you are working with." Certainly, the brochure is your bragging tool, but it is so much more acceptable when the prospective client or referral source reads it rather than you telling them how wonderful you are. Be certain that it presents a favorable image of you and has a professional appearance.

If you are new to the territory, this brochure can be mailed to the agents along with an introductory letter from a top official of your company or it can be accompanied by a letter from you. Regardless of how you use it, the brochure is one of the most effective marketing tools available to the mortgage loan officer. When it is mailed, be certain to include a few of your business cards along with your letter. Just remember, you are not very likely to get business just from the brochure; nor from advertising, marketing letters, rate sheets, etc. These are just part of a marketing "full court press" to develop awareness of you and what you have to offer. You are simply laying the foundation upon which your business relationships are built.

In addition to the distribution of your brochure to real estate agents, builders and other business referral sources it would be worthwhile to run selected segments as an advertisement in the local "homes for sale" magazines that are used by real estate brokers to advertise their listings.

These magazines are usually an excellent place to advertise because they reach the real estate agents and the buying public. The advertising is usually priced very reasonably. You can also expand your reach by placing the ad in a local community newspaper. For maximum effect always include your photo and use a similar format for all advertising as the continuity helps build and engrain your personal brand in the mind of referral sources and the public.

Like any marketing material or advertising, be certain it is in color and professionally prepared to create the greatest favorable impact. This does not mean that you cannot do the work yourself. It simply means that the quality of the work must be very high. Remember, if you go to the expense of preparing this marketing piece, be certain that you create a positive impression.

The marketing medium most frequently used by mortgage loan officers is the rate sheet. There is considerable debate as to the value of rate sheets, and with good reason. In a study by a major real estate organization, rate sheets had a useful life in the real estate office of less than fifteen minutes about 85% of the time. When they are used, they are often used to disqualify a lender due to rates that are too high. They are more frequently used as scrap note paper.

Rates sheets can be used effectively if they are not relied upon as your sole sales presentation. All too often, a loan officer will make a stealth sales call by running into a real estate office, drop off some rate sheets and leave without ever talking with a sales agent. That is not a sales call. That is a delivery service. In fact, if you use rate sheets as a marketing medium use a delivery service to take them to real estate offices once each week, preferably on Friday as your time is too valuable. More effectively, email them to your agents and save a tree as well as a lot of work on your part. Of course, take a few printed rate sheets with you when you are making sales calls so that you can hand them directly to the agents with whom you are meeting. Print your rate sheets each Friday and use that same sheet as a hand-out until the following Friday. That way you can shave a little off your rates to make them more attractive and explain to people that rates may have adjusted since the rate sheets were printed. Make certain the format of the rate sheet is clean and easy to read. Print them in color and always include your photo. Include the APR on the rate sheets so that they can be distributed to sources who are not real estate agents or brokers.

A hand-out that is generally more effective than the rate sheet is a product description flyer. This sheet is used to highlight a special loan program or attractive features of a standard program. If you have a special program or an interest rate that is worth showcasing, this is how it should be presented. If you take the time to indicate the advantages of this program over other competing programs (without naming the competitor's program) and some specific situations where this program could be beneficial, these sheets can be very productive for you. Use bullet points for the salient features. Keep the sheet "clean" and easy to read. Naturally you don't want to give them all the information because you want to encourage the real estate agents to call you for details. Be certain to include the product name or code so the real estate agent can look for it on your regular rate sheet or be able to identify the program if they call you for details. Of greatest importance is that the product hand out have the same border format with your photo as your rate sheets. Remember continuity in marketing is critical to building your personal brand.

Effective marketing must include use of the available news media both in terms of paid advertising and free notices. Use news releases to announce your appointment as a loan officer to a new territory or promotion to a new title or position. Use them to announce any certification or awards that you received, courses completed and community service performed. Every publication in your market should be provided with your news release along with your photograph.

All too often, this free avenue for promoting yourself and keeping your name and face in front of the real estate community is ignored. And while it is generally not as effective as other methods of promotion, it is part of an overall marketing plan and should not be overlooked. Be certain to talk with each publication in advance to determine what they require in order to publish your news release. Often they want you to be an advertiser with them in order to provide more than cursory reference to your release.

Throughout most of this book, a focus is placed on the loan officer's relationship with real estate agents and builders. They are certainly your primary avenues for referral business and much of your marketing will be directed toward them. But you also need to consider that every other loan officer is also aware of the business potential available from these sources so they are inundated with loan officers. If you have any doubt, sit in a real estate office for a few hours and watch the parade of loan officers that stream through. For this reason, you need to differentiate yourself from your competition.

You also need to focus some of your marketing effort on alternative business referral sources. While alternate sources will generally not provide you with as much business as those who build and sell real estate, there is less competition for their attention; and cumulatively, they could be an exceptional resource for a large portion of your loan business.

Chapter 15
Supplemental Marketing Strategies

Now that you have developed a comprehensive marketing plan and a powerful database you can use it to address envelopes and prepare letters, brochures and every other type of marketing material.

When you are sending a card, and there are always occasions to send cards, be certain to personally sign each one. Use only your first name when you sign the card because it seems much more personal, but drop a business card inside just in case they may not recognize you by your first name.

Since you should avoid religious holidays, you may be thinking what holidays may be appropriate to send a card. Take your pick, but note that some of the holidays listed below occur on different days each year. But, since you will probably be mailing a card about five days in advance of the event, it probably doesn't matter a great deal whether you have the specific date. However, it you are a detail oriented person you may check the calendar before the start of the new-year and adjust the dates for that year.

Here are the dates from 2010:
(Keep in mind that many dates change from year to year)

- *New Year (1st of January)*
- *Groundhog Day (2nd of February)*
- Martin Luther King Day (3rd Monday in January)
- Super Bowl (7th of February)
- Lincoln's Birthday (12th of February)
- Valentine's Day (14th of February)
- Lunar New Year (14th of February)
- President's Day (3rd Monday in February)
- Washington's Birthday (22nd of February)
- *Daylight Saving Time Begins (2nd Sunday in March)*
- St. Patrick's Day (17th of March)
- Spring Equinox (20th of March)
- April Fools Day (1st of April)
- *Earth Day (22nd of April)*
- Law Day (1st of May)
- *Cinco de Mayo (5th of May)*
- Mother's Day (2nd Sunday in May)
- Armed Forces Day (17th of May)
- Memorial Day (Last Monday in May)
- Flag Day (14th of June)
- Father's Day (3rd Sunday in June)
- *Garfield's Birthday (18th of June)*
- Summer Solstice (21st of June)
- *Independence Day (4th of July)*
- Bastille Day (14th of July)
- *National Ice Cream Day (19th of July)*
- Labor Day (1st of September)
- Grandparents Day (First Sunday in September after Labor Day)
- *Fall Equinox (23rd of September)*
- Columbus Day (2nd Monday in October)
- United Nations Day (24th of October)
- *Halloween (31st of October)*
- *Daylight Saving Time Ends (1st Sunday of November)*
- Election Day (First Tuesday after the first Monday of November)
- Veteran's Day (11th of November)
- *Thanksgiving (4th Thursday in November)*
- *Boston Tea Party Day (16th of December)*
- Winter Solstice (21st of December)
- New Year's Eve (31st of December)

The holidays in bold italics are relatively safe for marketing and spaced throughout the year. The other holidays can be useful for any number of purposes including a humorous reminder that your office will be offering a special rebate of $500 toward closing costs in recognition of Groundhog Day or gift certificates for ice cream at the local ice cream emporium during National Ice Cream Month (July), for example. Keep in mind that the idea of the cards for these holidays is simply to keep your name and face in front of the agents and other referral sources and to have an excuse to do so. Be creative and have fun, but watch the budget.

Please note that all holidays are state designated holidays (there is no such thing as a "National Holiday") although there are "Federal Holidays," when the U.S. government observes a holiday. Some holidays are recognized by all the states, but each state makes the decision as to the holidays that will be observed in its jurisdiction. Your state may have some special days that should be included on your holiday list.

Not only can you use these holidays to send a card, you can also use them as themes for trinkets. Of course some items are more expensive than others but here are some things that you can distribute to your referral sources whether there is a "major holiday" or not. Naturally, everything should have your name, company name, your cell phone number, email address and web address or at least as much information as will fit on the product.

Here are some things that you can distribute to your referral sources:

Ball point pens (preferably "click" style)
Note pads or Post-it-Notes®
Coupons for a $500 closing cost credit (use a different dollar amount if you prefer and be certain that each coupon has an expiration date and the phrase "not valid with any other offer")
Local sports team schedule
NFL football team schedules
Inflatable beach balls at the beginning of summer
Miniature foam basketballs during basketball season or during the NCAA tournament
Miniature foam baseballs during baseball season
Miniature foam footballs when the fall football season begins
Coupons to an ice cream store in July for National Ice Cream Month
Birthday cupcake (with one unlit candle) for an agent's birthday

If you take a cupcake to a referral client for their birthday then others in their office may expect one for their birthday. Simply tell them if they send mortgage referrals to you then you will be happy to help them celebrate their birthday. With the more expensive items, consider alternating with footballs one year, baseballs the next, beach balls the following year and basketballs the fourth year, etc. If the agents know it is only for your referral sources it may be just enough to encourage some new agents to send you some business. Remember, the primary reason for these gifts is to bring you to the attention of agents who are not sending business to you.

Be careful about the cost and number of items you give away. The expense can be daunting if you are marketing to a large number of agents. In a law office or the office of an accountant, financial planner or other professional you may be well served to deliver the birthday cupcake to the clerical employee who is celebrating a birthday rather than your referral source. The reason you give things away is to generate some recognition and get business referrals. Give a great deal of thought to how you can best leverage your marketing dollars. This is one of the primary reasons that you need to develop a marketing plan before you begin marketing your services.

You should offer goodies as judiciously as possible. Otherwise, you can spend every income dollar to support your philanthropy. Also keep in mind that there is no real requirement that you give anything away. After all, your immeasurable competence in getting their buyer's mortgage approved should be more than enough. You may have already made a difference of several thousand dollars in their income. That is why they should choose you as their mortgage banker and that should be enough.

Chapter 16
Cost Considerations

There are an unlimited number of opportunities for you to spend money promoting your mortgage banking practice. Success always has a cost and money is one of the most obvious. Of course, there are other costs in the form of personal sacrifice of your time, consumption of your energy, reduction in time with family and friends. But here, the issue is money.

As a new loan officer, you may not have tens of thousands of dollars to invest in your career. Even if you do, judicious spending is critical, both in your personal life and in the promotion of your professional mortgage banking career.

There is an old saying: "It takes money to make money." It also takes effort and many personal sacrifices to make money. So, when starting or re-energizing your career as a mortgage banker, start with the resources that you have in the greatest abundance. At the beginning of your career you will have more time and energy to commit to your career but probably limited amounts of money. As your career matures, your time will be more constrained by the demands of high loan volume but money will be more plentiful.

Start the process by preparing a budget. What things do you need to start your career? You will certainly need a computer, but you may already have one or, if not, your employer may provide a computer. You will also need a suitable business wardrobe. That is something that is critical that your employer will not provide.

Of course you will need serviceable transportation but an expensive luxury car is not necessary. If you cannot afford a new or newer used car you can get by with an older car. However, accurately or not, your referral sources may judge your competence by your perceived level of financial success so that an old, beat-up car can be a negative factor, if they see it. You are far better served to keep the older car and park it out of sight away from the referral sources office than to put yourself in debt to buy a new car. In time that shiny new car will be very affordable.

When you have spent a lifetime looking at the financial picture of thousands of borrowers it becomes abundantly clear that the difference in their prosperity is only minimally related to their income and profoundly related to their level of debt or, in the best case, their total absence of debt. The lessons of this book are focused on helping you generate a large income so don't waste your hard earned money on things you don't need, or worse, on interest payment on loans and credit cards that simply erode your income and assets. There are only three things in life that are worth intentionally incurring debt: #1. Student loan for a college education; #2. Mortgage to buy a home (of course) and, #3. A loan to buy a car, but only if it is essential to get you to and from your job. Debt is financial death. It is surprising how inexpensively you can live when you are debt free.

Develop a budget and a financial plan for both your personal and your professional life. Here, the focus will be on the business element of your finances, but it all reflects back to your personal financial position.

106

Determine exactly what your employer is willing to subsidize to help you generate business. Here is a quick list of possible expense items:

1. Business computer – A laptop is better than a desk top computer because of its portability
2. Memberships (industry organizations): Realtors® Association, builders association, mortgage bankers / mortgage brokers organizations
3. Memberships (community organizations): Civic groups such as Jaycees, Kiwanis, Rotary, Exchange Club, Chamber of Commerce, and other organizations within the community
4. Sponsorships for charitable organizations or charitable events
5. Participation in local or regional annual events, such as a "Founders Day" or "City Festival," etc.
6. Professional photograph of you for use on promotional material
7. Printing, postage, letterhead, envelopes and paper for brochures and mailings
8. Company provided website where borrowers can input mortgage application information where the data comes directly to you not to a company processing center where you get no credit for the production
9. Print advertisements in real estate magazines, community newspapers or other local and regional publications
10. Lunch or dinner to entertain viable referral sources
11. Snack food if you are giving a presentation to a sales meeting of real estate agents

12. Flowers for agents or real estate offices as a "thank you" for business

13. Tickets to sporting events, concerts, etc. as an expression of thanks for cumulative business that they have sent to you. Unless you have an unavoidable conflict, always accompany your referral clients to these events in order to cement your relationship with them; don't just give tickets to them unless you can't possibly attend the event and when possible, include spouses, yours and theirs.

14. Trinkets – Small, inexpensive "give away" items such as pens, note pads, post-it notes, etc. These should all have your name, company name, phone number, email address and web address if space permits.

15. Event related items – For events like the NCAA basketball tournament you can give away small foam replica basketballs; and similar items prior to the football season, baseball season, or inflatable beach balls at the beginning of summer. All of these items should have your name, phone number, email address and web address if space permits. You might distribute flags for July 4th or candy for Halloween. You can even give agents party hats or noise makers (at your own risk) for New Years. Stay far, far away from religious holidays.

These items can be expensive so plan accordingly. Leverage what your employer will pay and minimize your contribution until your production makes these investments in your career a little more affordable. Check the prices at several business gift stores or similar websites and order the items at least two months in advance of the date you plan to distribute them just to be absolutely certain that you get them on time. If you are distributing Halloween candy at the end of November you will not be able to pass it off as a Thanksgiving treat and everyone will assume that you gave your favored clients Halloween candy on time and that you are just getting around to distributing the left-over candy to unimportant agents. Or, even worse, that you are too poorly organized to get things done on time, such as loan approvals.

Often when you are distributing goodies to your regular referral agents someone in the office from whom you have not received any business may ask if they can have one too, particularly the basketballs and footballs; the answer is always "yes" because you look like a jerk if you say "no." This is a good opportunity for an introduction to some potential new referral sources. However, be certain to get their business card and then tell them as you give them the valued item that they owe you a couple good loan referrals. As always send them a nice handwritten "nice to meet you" note afterward with the notation that you look forward to working with them and their homebuyers.

Check the MLS sales volume records to determine whether this agent is worth pursuing as a primary or secondary level agent. At least keep them on your email distribution list regardless of their stature as an agent and follow up with them if you haven't received a mortgage referral within 45 days. They owe it to you; that was the agreement for which they received the item they coveted. You may be a nice person but you are not a charitable foundation; you deserve to be compensated for what you do.

After you have determined what contribution your employer will make toward your potential expenses, prepare your budget. Determine how much you can afford to invest each month for the business gifts and other marketing activities which you have chosen. When you determine how many basketballs you can afford to purchase, you may conclude that you can't give them to all your referral clients. So you should distribute them only to the agents that have already referred business to you and those top priority agents with whom you want to develop a business relationship. You may also decide that you should distribute less expensive trinkets or perhaps nothing at all. The side benefit of giving something to the top agents is that some agents will presume that the top producing agents to whom you gave gifts are referring buyers to you. That adds to your credibility in the office. Always order twice what you plan to give away. As the event gets closer and if you still have some items left then you can selectively distribute them to some additional agents. This is a serious business so you need to keep good records so that you know where your money is best invested and whether there is a financial return from "gifting" the agents.

Take the agents who send you business on a regular basis to lunch or send them flowers. On more than one occasion I have been in a real estate office to meet an agent for lunch and I have been asked by another agent when I am taking them to lunch. My response is that we will go to lunch to celebrate the next closing with one of our mutual clients. In other words, when you send me a loan I will take you to lunch. Unless the agent is one of my primary targeted agents from whom I haven't yet received business, I won't take an agent to lunch as a speculative investment. It is virtually always an appreciation lunch. The exception is the top producing agent with the potential for sending a lot of business my way. You won't buy them off with a lunch but you can start developing a good business relationship that can be mutually beneficial. This business is all about relationships; build many long, deep relationships with agents and you will be highly successful.

Chapter 17
Real Estate Agent Referrals

Real estate agents are easy to find, but determining who the productive agents are may take a little more work. If possible, get the entire state's database of licensed real estate agents and brokers in electronic form and update it annually. Then obtain the sales volume data from the local Realtor® Association or the multiple listing service. This information will help you identify the agents you should be pursuing for business. Match the production volume to the agents in your database.

The biggest challenge most mortgage loan officers face is getting access to real estate offices. Certainly you can just drop-in and introduce yourself to the sales agents who happen to be in the office, but there is a much better way. After you have built your database and you have your list of real estate offices in your designated territory, simply call each office on the phone, introduce yourself to the person who answers with your name and the company you represent and ask who the managing broker of that office is. Then, ask if you may speak with that person. When the managing broker answers, again introduce yourself and then tell them that you are a mortgage banker who provides financing in their area and since you expect to handle transactions for agents in that office or if you are already providing financing for their agents, you thought it would be a good idea to stop by and introduce yourself. Then arrange a convenient time to go in and meet the managing broker. Don't suggest that you want to schedule a "meeting" or an "appointment" because that sounds too formal, all you want to do is "stop by" to introduce yourself.

If the managing broker is not available when you call for an appointment, you will probably be asked if you would like to leave a message. Tell the person "no" and that you will call again at another time. Thank them for their courtesy and hang-up. The reason you don't want to leave a message is that the broker may not return your call and then you are left to call again and potentially leave another message. At that point you start to look like a stalker. Besides, it is always more convenient for you to talk with the managing broker on your schedule, when you have time to call them. The next time you call you will know the name of the person who you need to speak with and that improves the likelihood of getting through to them. When you make phone calls, before you say anything else, always tell the person who you are and then ask for the person to whom you want to talk.

At your meeting with the managing broker, ask them if they have any particular policies regarding mortgage loan officers and the referral of clients for financing. Tell them a little about yourself and your mortgage banking experience. Then, give them a copy of your "Introducing Your Mortgage Banker" brochure while asking if you may have a list of the agents in that office. Sometimes they will decline or tell you that they don't have a list available.

In some states there are laws that require real estate firms have a list of agents available for anyone who asks. Simply mention that you are certain they must have a list someplace since the state laws require them to have a list available. If there is no such law or they otherwise decline to provide a list, you can mention that you know that the state requires that the license of each sales agent be posted in the office so ask if you may see the posted licenses.

If you must use the posted licenses to get the agent's names, be sure to take your time and write down every individual's name and be very careful that you spell the name correctly for your records. Don't be rushed by the managing broker standing there waiting for you to finish. This is too important to rush. Then, ask the managing broker if they would be kind enough to introduce you to the agents who are in the office while you are there. In many cases the managing broker will be very cordial and accommodating with regard to providing the names of their agents and introduce you to those agents in the office during your visit. When being introduced to agents, be certain to give every agent two or three of your business cards and ask for one of their cards.

The references to state laws and posted licenses are offered here simply as fall-back options. You want your relationship with all the agents and particularly the managing broker to be very cordial so make every effort to avoid a confrontational situation where you are demanding information and threatening them with the rule of law. But, on the other hand be certain that you get the names of all the agents; just be polite.

Sometimes the managing broker will simply tell you that they generally don't allow individuals seeking business such as loan officers, title companies, office supply businesses, etc. access to the office as it is disruptive for the agents. Tell them that you understand but that you want to be sure that it is OK for you to come in the office if you have a scheduled meeting with one of their agents. This will clarify the situation so that when you are in the office visiting their agents there will be no issue that you are circumventing the company's rules.

Over the years there have been a lot of schemes recommended by people training loan officers on how to get past the receptionist and into the office where the agents are located. Some of these techniques will work, but the problem is that everyone in the office understands that you got there by using some form of subterfuge. That undermines your credibility. It may even foster a level of distain for you that may never be overcome. You may be viewed as sneaky, dishonest and not worthy of their trust and most certainly not worthy of business from their clients. If you violated their rules, even the agents who may otherwise be inclined to work with you will be discouraged because of peer pressure from the other agents.

Following your visit to each real estate office, send everyone you met a personal handwritten note card telling them how nice it was to meet them, including the managing broker. Be sure to do it the same day, probably in the evening. For those agents who were not in the office send them a handwritten note card telling them how disappointed you are that you did not have the opportunity to meet them while you were in the office and that you look forward to meeting them soon. Naturally, you should include two or three business cards with each note card. Then, update your database by matching the agents in that office with those in your database and include any relevant information that you gleaned from your visit.

The offices where it is difficult to gain access could become your most productive accounts. If it is difficult for you to gain access, then it is probably difficult for every other mortgage banker to gain access unless one of their close relatives owns the company.

These businesses can ultimately be some of your best accounts if you are persistent, because every other loan officer will have been scared off or simply given up and there won't be much competition for their referrals. Sometimes it is difficult to determine whether an account is a well guarded treasure or a waste of time. Don't give up too quickly, but don't keep going back every week for five years without getting some business from the account. If you aren't getting business after a couple months, be certain to ask why. Keep in mind that if you can't get in the door past the receptionist, you can phone the office and simply ask for specific individuals; after all, you have their names from the licensing authority. Yes, you do need to be assertive, but always be diplomatic and polite.

With your database up-to-date with all the names of every agent in each real estate office in your area you are in a great position to send occasional mail merge letters, postcards, newsletters, flyers or anything else you would like to send. Occasionally sort your database by birthdays so that you can prepare birthday cards to be mailed to agents about five days prior to their birthday. Send the cards to the office rather than their home, because if you send it to their home the agent's spouse may be a little irritated if they see a birthday card from a loan officer. Of course, there is the added benefit of sending the card to the office when other agents in the office see that someone got a birthday card from you. It makes you seem like a genuinely nice person and it raises your profile in that office. Many agents will look forward to receiving their card. Birthday cards should be real cards, not e-cards because no one else in the office is likely to see an e-card and your objective is to create awareness.

All birthday cards, as well as cards for other special events, should have a humorous content, unless of course your card is one of condolence for a death or other distressing event in their family. In that case, you should either send a more serious and appropriate card or send a personal handwritten note card expressing your condolences. Sending cards of this nature to the agent's home or office is acceptable.

The cultivation of agents must be undertaken with a sense of purpose and with great persistence. A phone call once each year simply isn't enough. Initially, you need to have a personal meeting with every agent in your database. This is how you get to know them on a personal level and how they get to know you. Certainly, you need to talk about business and how the two of you can work together to build your mutual business practices, but a large portion of the conversation will be about the personal things that are important to the agent. Of course some agents don't care to reveal any of their personal lives and you will probably sense that very early in the conversation. Still, take a couple minutes to tell them something relevant about you such as growing up in the area or, if you know that they live in your neighborhood or in the neighborhood of your relatives, be certain to mention that, but then move on to business-related matters. Most relationships develop over time and some simply require more time than others.

In most cases, you should not spend more than fifteen or twenty minutes with each agent and only meet with one agent in an office at a time. If you schedule meetings with half-a-dozen agents from the same office, it will look like an assembly line event rather than the personal relationship building process that it is intended to be. It will be far less efficient to only meet with one agent on each visit, but in the long run it will be far more productive. Besides, it gives you a reason to be back in that real estate office on a regular basis to meet with each of the other agents. You can still have a few casual conversations with other agents while you are there, but don't stay too long as it will appear that you have nothing else to do but loiter in their office. You want to appear busy as successful mortgage bankers are busy and don't have time to waste. Remember, perception is reality, so if they think that you are busy then they will perceive you to be successful and your success must be because of your exemplary service to clients.

Before each agent meeting you definitely need to review the information that you have on the agent as that is the reason you keep a database. Following the meeting with each agent, sit down and extract information from your notes and memory of the meeting and put the relevant information in your database. Then, write a nice handwritten note to the agent telling them how nice it was talking with them and that you look forward to working with them to assist your mutual clients.

Because many agents now work from their home, you may not have the opportunity to meet every agent while visiting the real estate office with which they are affiliated. The managing broker of each office should be able to tell you which agents work from home and which ones are part-time agents who may have little or no business. For these agents, you can send material directly to their home or call them in the evening to create contact. Just be careful of interrupting their time with their family as well as the recognizing that the ones who are part-time agents are unlikely to be significant sources of business.

Now that you have had an introduction to the agents, either in person or by note card, you have an opening to call them, drop in to deliver a brochure on a new product or invite them to an event. Just be certain that you always have a reason to contact them. Just calling to say "hi" will not be appreciated by agents who are busy, but you can call them and ask what they are working on and ask how you can help them. Offer to assist them at an open house. This gives you time to bond with the agent and meet a number of prospective borrowers who may end up buying through them or another real estate agent. If you hold a real estate license you may even consider asking the agent if you may hold the open house yourself on behalf of the real estate agent. In most jurisdictions, you cannot discuss information related to the house unless you have a real estate license. You can, of course, provide each prospect with a printed brochure on the property and naturally, discuss mortgage financing matters. The open house can be a double edge sword, although it helps you develop the relationship with the real estate agent it can also give the impression that you have nothing else to do which could be interpreted as you aren't getting much business which may imply that you may not be a very good loan officer. However, you can justify having the time since most open houses are on weekends.

You should consider joining the local Realtors® Association so that you can get access to their membership list. This list will often have email addresses which can be very useful and an important element of your database. In some cases you may also need to join the separate multiple listing service to get some of this information. Before you join these or any other organization, be sure to confirm what information will be available to you. You don't want to pay several hundred dollars to join an organization for which you get no value. If you hold a real estate license, you can more easily gain access to some of the Realtor® membership lists. Of course, some real estate associations actually post their entire membership list on their web site. Do your research before spending money as there will be plenty of other opportunities to spend it.

When building your database you can often get some of the information from the agent's website and from ads they run in newspapers and local real estate magazines. Business volume data is often available from the local multiple listing service. Many real estate firms also run large ads at least once each year listing all their top sales and listing agents. This is an excellent resource for identifying the agents that you should designate as your primary or secondary targeted agents. Don't wait until the next ads appear in the newspaper; check the library for back issues or the "morgue" of your local newspaper. It will typically be in the weekly real estate section of the newspaper. Some real estate offices and agents post the ad in their office and while you probably can't sit there and copy the information, you can see the date that the ad was run so that you know where to find it.

You will learn the most about your agents when you sit down and talk with them. Be diplomatic about how you gather information. For example, don't ask for the names of their children, but you can ask the ages of their children and they may volunteer more such as gender and name. Whatever you do, don't be seen writing down the names of their children as it will seem a little strange. Make these notes in your notebook after you return to your car from what you can remember from the conversation. Anything that you forget can be retrieved during your next visit with the agent.

When you refer a buyer to a real estate agent, the agent may tell you that they will make every effort to see that any buyers referred to them use you for the mortgage. However, they may not agree to refer other business. In the most basic of commission arrangements real estate agents receive 50% of the brokerage fee received by their company (typically 1½% on a total 6% commission) and the loan officer receives 50 basis points on the smaller loan.

The real estate agent makes a minimum of three times what the loan officer makes from that same transaction and often as much as six times the loan officer's income. Therefore, at a minimum, the agent should not only be certain that the loan officer gets that first transaction but at least two more just to break even. Don't be shy to point that out to the agent, because it makes it clear that they owe you more valid referrals. Besides, it costs them nothing to refer business to you. In addition, you are a great support system for that agent by assuring their buyer that they have purchased a wonderful property at a great price and that they are very fortunate to be working with that particular real estate agent. That should generate more referrals to the agent from that client. You are worth money to that agent so don't forget to tell them; diplomatically, of course.

In your role as a mortgage banker, you must emphasize to the real estate agent the value of their time and that the most successful agents always make certain that every prospective borrower is qualified for financing before investing time in showing property to them. An important side benefit of having you pre-approve every prospective buyer is that you will have identity documentation for everyone and that is important protection for the agent, guarding them against the risk of working with anonymous prospects that may pose a physical risk to the agent.

Every agent should call you with each prospective buyer's name and phone number so that you can contact them and get them pre-approved. As a professional mortgage banker, this means that you obtain their pay-stubs, W-2 forms, bank statements and a tri-merged credit report along with any other documentation that will be needed to get the loan approved. Of course some of those items may not be needed if they qualify for a loan with limited documentation, but be certain that you have absolutely everything that you would need for a complete approval.

It is prudent to ask for everything you could possibly need from a borrower even though some items may ultimately not be required. Everyone, including the borrower and the referral source, detest it when a lender keeps asking for more support documents. Ask and get everything up front because sometimes the documentation can raise questions that must be resolved before a loan can be offered. Give every borrower a written checklist of exactly what documentation they need to provide to obtain a pre-approval letter. Do not, under any circumstances, produce a pre-approval letter if documentation is still outstanding.

The very last thing you ever want to do is an old style "pre-qualification" based on unverified information provided by the prospective clients. If you don't verify the qualifying information and the agent spends time with the potential buyer, finds them a property, negotiates a contract and then finds out that the client doesn't actually qualify to purchase the home, then you need to buy another book on how to prepare for your next career. An absolute reality in this business is that a satisfied real estate agent may never mention to anyone about the spectacular job you did in handling a difficult or complex transaction, but an agent who is angry over a poorly handled transaction will tell everyone and tell them at least three times, with special audible emphasis on your name so that everyone within at least a hundred yards can hear about how incompetent you are. And it really doesn't matter whether it was your fault or you were essentially the victim; you will bear the burden of the blame.

Most real estate transactions involve two agents who are often associated with two separate real estate brokerage firms. Use this opportunity to leverage this connection and talk with each agent involved. As long as there is no conflict with your company's "territory" policy, build your relationship with this additional agent. After the transaction settles, call that agent's managing broker and do exactly the same thing you would do with any other new real estate office. Except in this case you already have a contact and a great reference in this office.

What about making a presentation at a real estate company's sales meeting? This is a great opportunity to show how knowledgeable you are and to be presented to all the agents of a real estate firm as a true mortgage banking expert. Just be certain that you are providing them with information that has value and that you aren't just presenting a mortgage banking "commercial" amid their office sales meeting. You can use issues such as a change in mortgage lending laws or loan guidelines at Fannie Mae or Freddie Mac or the government agencies. Getting the opportunity to make the presentation is something that virtually every loan officer wants, but find that it is hard to get. This is where your relationship with the managing broker at each office will pay dividends as you can call them directly and tell them that you would like to take a few minutes at one of their next sales meetings to tell them about the recent developments in lending.

If you have a real estate license you may consider contacting a local community college about teaching the licensing courses for real estate agents and brokers. This is a great opportunity to be presented as the first mortgage lending expert that the new agents will be exposed to. Since these courses usually run for several weeks you will have the opportunity to develop great relationships with these new agents and brokers. Just be certain that you have studied all the material before each class and that you have a good lesson plan for each session. While this is a wonderful opportunity to look like the mortgage expert, you can also come across as the mortgage idiot if you are not prepared.

At this point you are probably thinking that this is really a lot of work. Yes it is. But realize that hard work is essential to success in every profession. All you have to do is follow the work plan that is being described and you will earn a very healthy income. You can work hard, play hard, and be rich.

Chapter 18
Builders & Developers

In addition to real estate agents, the other most obvious source of mortgage referrals is builders of single family homes and their sales agents. In many areas builders employ real estate firms to market their properties, while in other areas it is more common for the builder to have their own sales staff.

Relationships with successful builders can be worth their weight in gold. The value comes in the fact that once the relationship is established, there can continue to be a stream of business without the frequent sales calls that may be necessary with real estate sales agents although regular contact is still essential. Builders want to focus on building homes rather than fussing over financing. And, if you provide the construction financing, you may get two loans and two commission checks for each borrower.

Builders can be more demanding than real estate agents because they have more riding on each transaction, but the business that results can be well worth the extra effort. While the real estate agent is concerned about their commission check, the builder is concerned about the profit margin. Since most builders don't receive most of their profit until the property is sold and closed, they are anxious for the transaction to be settled as soon as construction is complete. Another factor of concern to the builder is that interest on the construction loan continues to accrue until the sale is closed and the construction loan is paid off. The longer the construction interest accrues the less profit the builder makes on the house. Therefore, a prompt closing is critical to retaining builders as clients. You need to be prepared to close on the financing no later than the day after the builder obtains the certificate of occupancy or its equivalent. You must, therefore, closely monitor construction progress of each home.

If you plan to seek business from a builder, go prepared. Be certain you can provide a list of references who will speak very favorably of their mortgage lending experience with you. It is beneficial if you can provide copies of reference letters from real estate agents, buyers, sellers or anyone else who has been involved in a transaction with you, particularly other builders. Put this information together in a binder with a nice cover along with a brief summary of your experience, some information about your company and information about your loan programs. Don't include your rates or fees, but be prepared to discuss them in detail during your meeting.

Unlike real estate agents where you can walk in without an appointment, be sure to call the builder in advance to arrange a convenient time to meet with them. But before you make that call, compose a good short letter stating that you have some excellent builder finance programs that you feel would be beneficial to the builder and briefly tell them why. For example, be sure to tell them if you are able to provide a "one time close loan" or a pre-approval of a buyer that is valid until the home is complete, regardless of changes in the borrower's employment, income, credit, etc. This would mean that the builder has a firm buyer with a binding contract without the usual provision that makes the transaction subject to a buyer having to "re-qualify" by having their documentation updated before closing. This has value to a builder.

It is important for a builder to know that they have a firm sale, because they occasionally get buyers who qualify when the contract is first written but don't qualify when the mortgage documents are up-dated as the house nears completion. Sometimes this happens because the borrower has lost a job or because a credit problem has surfaced, or because the buyer went out and bought a new car with a high payment that pushed their ratios too high. Whatever the reason, this situation can leave the builder with a nearly built house and no qualified buyer.

Maybe you offer a program with one closing for the construction and permanent financing where the financing is all in the name of the borrower rather than the builder. This means that the builder doesn't have to use their line of credit to build the house. If you have a solution that could benefit the builder, be certain that the builder knows how you can help them.

Be sure to specify the key advantage of any loan program or feature that you offer. You can allude to other advantages too, but do not make the letter too long. Keep it to less than a single page. Also state in the letter, that you will be calling to arrange a time to discuss the financing programs you offer and explore whether they may be beneficial to the builder. You should probably not specify when you will call, but simply state that you will call them "next week" or some other vague time. Be sure to include your "Mortgage Banker" brochure.

If your firm provides construction financing, you have the perfect opportunity to exploit this market by tying the end loans to the construction loan agreement. But, even if you do not have construction financing available, you can still access this market for permanent financing.

While it is rare, some builders obtain their constructions funds from lenders who don't offer end loan financing such as a small local bank so the door is open to any mortgage lender to provide the permanent financing for their buyers. In these cases, you should develop a relationship with the construction lender and that will help you get other referrals.

If the construction lender does not provide end loans, they may not be too anxious to have another lender involved with the project that provides both end loans and construction financing. If you provide only end loan financing, they may be very supportive of your efforts so that they can maintain their construction lending relationship with the builder unimpeded by another lender that may provide both the construction funds as well as end loans.

Before you approach a builder check the public records to see which lender has recorded construction loans on their projects. This will tell you who your competition may be. Also look at which lender has recorded permanent loans on homes sold by the builder. If most financing is with one lender then you will have a pretty good idea who is providing permanent financing. If you find that there are numerous permanent lenders listed it may mean that the builder leaves each buyer to find their own financing or it could mean that the builder is using a mortgage broker who sells loans to several wholesale lenders. Either way, when you tell them what you noticed from the public records they will recognize that you are a competent professional mortgage banker who does their homework.

Most builders see financing and sales as two necessary impediments to what they really want to do, which is build houses. If you can show them how you can help them alleviate the financing issue, then you have a great opportunity to develop a good business relationship with the builder.

Chapter 19
Ancillary Housing Industry Business Sources

Although real estate brokers and sales agents are the primary source of business from the housing industry, quickly followed by builders of single family homes, there are other affiliated businesses that can also be a source of mortgage referrals.

Relocation companies are a conduit to the buyers that real estate agents prize the most. These are the buyers who must move because of a transfer by their employer. This makes them far more attractive to the real estate agents than the prospective buyer who currently lives in town and who may or may not move. On the negative side, relocation companies often demand referral fees up to 35% of the real estate company's brokerage fee. This often causes the top agents to demur when offered relocation referrals because they have other sources of business from which they can earn full fees. But there are always agents willing to accept the lower fees for higher quality business.

From the lenders perspective, what makes the relocation buyers so attractive is the support their employer is providing for the transfer. These employees generally have good job stability and excellent future employment prospects. Their companies usually pay the closing cost and sometimes subsidize the mortgage payments. Because most transferees are under some time pressure to buy and close on a home, they generally don't commit a great deal of time for shopping around for mortgage rates. However, large companies often negotiate special financing terms with major lenders which could mean that the loan goes to another lender or to a corporate relocation department in your company. Neither option benefits you. But you won't know until you make a sales call on the relocation company or the relocation department of real estate brokerage firms. Hockey star Wayne Gretzky said "You miss 100% of the shots you don't take." That is exactly where you are now, so you truly have everything to gain and nothing to lose by taking your shot, because the worst that can happen is that they tell you "no." But they may also say "yes" and you have discovered a great new source of business.

The challenging side of handling corporate relocation business is where the transferee's spouse has been employed and the couple depends on both incomes for their mortgage payment. Unless the spouse has already arranged for a job in the new location, there could be a problem getting this buyer to qualify. If your company gives consideration for a "trailing spouse's" income, you could have a distinct advantage in working with corporate relocations. If not, this could be an obstacle, but it should not be impossible to overcome. While it is not your role to find jobs for clients, at least ask for their resume and see if you can make some contacts on their behalf. This is one place where your membership in local civic groups, such as the Chamber of Commerce, can come in particularly handy. If you can arrange for the spouse to have an interview for a job, your efforts will be appreciated. If a job results, you will be loved by the borrower and their spouse. More importantly, your stature will be greatly elevated in the eyes of the builder or real estate agent involved in the transaction.

In some cases, companies that transfer employees provide help in finding a suitable position for the spouse of their employee, with some even providing for continuation of income for the spouse for a limited time or until the spouse finds a suitable position. These benefits, which alone do not help the employee and their spouse qualify for the loan, do offer compensating factors which could allow a loan to be approved prior to the spouse becoming employed, especially if the spouse has had a career in a profession that is in high demand.

In addition to the employee relocation companies, there are often departments in some of the larger real estate firms that specialize in relocation services. In these instances, determine who runs these departments and who makes the decisions regarding financing. Once you have identified the individuals who control these relocation departments, call on them with the same frequency that you would call on another top producing real estate agent.

Marketing your services to relocation companies and the relocation departments of real estate firms will require a lot of preparation similar to calling on a builder. Be sure you are well prepared and know which programs and services you can offer that would be appropriate and beneficial to these companies and their clients. The final decision on any financing lies with the borrower and, of course, the underwriter but you will need to be prepared to discuss a few appropriate loan products. You must also be able to talk about the process and time frame to get their relocation clients to settlement. Fast is good.

Another potential source of relocation business, though a little more difficult to cultivate, is the corporate human resource department. While they are involved with hiring and relocating employees, they are infrequently prepared to become involved in the home buying process. Generally the human resource department refers the employee to a relocation company or a real estate brokerage firm with which they have an agreement. Often they simply tell the employees to buy the house with their own financing and the company will reimburse appropriate expenses. If this is the case, ask the human resources department which real estate firm they use and the name of their contact at that company. Then, meet with that individual and ask them exactly what it will take for you to become their preferred mortgage lender.

Every company is slightly different in how they handle relocations, so over a period of time it will be worth your effort to contact the human resources department of each medium to large size company in your area to determine how they handle new hires and relocations. Companies that are large enough to handle the relocation of their own employees often have an agreement with a nationwide mortgage lender to provide the financing for the employees at a discounted rate so there may be no direct opportunity for you, but you may find a valuable new source of business. Even if you don't get mortgage referrals for the company's relocating employees you may get other business from other employees or the staff in the human resources department. You may consider offering an "employee financing plan" for all employees of a company where you offer reduced rates or fees to get their business. A small profit on a lot of loans is a lot of money. The company can then market the program as an employee benefit.

Architects may refer both builders and homeowners to you for financing if you take the time to cultivate them as a source of business. A distinct advantage here is that the individuals that architects design homes for generally build or remodel fairly large and expensive homes. Architects also design a lot of home additions and renovations and of course they design homes for builders. The important point is to have architects introduce you to their clients or to at least let you put brochures in their office for prospective borrowers.

If you can provide acquisition and development funds along with construction loans, you will definitely want to invest some time with land planners and engineers. Although they will generally not be the borrowers themselves, they are often in a position to influence the builders and developers with suggestions about who may provide financing for their projects.

Insurance agents who handle homeowners insurance are usually in contact with homeowners to keep their insurance coverage current. They may be aware of a client's intent to sell or buy real estate. This could be worth the time spent communicating with insurance agents in your area. Insurance agents will also look to loan officers to refer borrowers for their homeowner's insurance. When you recommend an insurance agent to a client, the payback can be beneficial.

There is one thing that you should always keep in mind as you talk to the individuals we have discussed in this section. While they may or may not be in a position to refer their employees or clients to you, they can always use your services themselves and refer their friends, relatives, colleagues and other associates to you. Always mention this to them; never leave it to them to think of it on their own.

Chapter 20
Direct Relationship Business

We all have friends, some more than others, but everyone knows a few people. That is all it takes. In fact, we all probably know more people than we think that we know. All too often we fail to recognize that everyone is a potential borrower as well as a prospective referral source. Consider the following list and think about all the people that you know, including everyone in your personal address book that fit into each of these categories:

° Family members (parents, grandparents, siblings, children, aunts, uncles, cousins, nieces, nephews, spouse's family, etc.)
° Personal friends, as well as friends & colleagues of your spouse or life partner
° Civic clubs where you are a member
° Health club / gym
° Community organizations
° PTA affiliations
° Parents of your children's friends and everyone they know
° Neighbors
° Personal business contacts, such as your dry cleaner, auto mechanic, hair stylist, grocery store clerks, personal physician, dentist, pharmacist, lawyer, accountant, financial planner, etc.

Among the non-traditional business sources are everyone you are in contact with every day such as the florist, dry cleaner, grocery store employees, the post office clerks, your child care provider, the landscape and lawn care service, the exterminator, plumber, electrician, religious congregation members, restaurant staff and your personal lawyer, accountant and financial planner.

Everyone with whom you have any business or personal relationship is a prospective borrower and a potential referral source. For example, if you leave your car with the dealer or a mechanic for repairs, simply give them one of your business card so that they have your phone number if they need to reach you to discuss that special, previously unknown and very expensive repair that your car must have. When you give them your card, simply tell them that "here is my phone number if you need to reach me...or if you need mortgage financing." This same idea holds true with everyone with whom you come in contact. They are all prospective customers as well as potential referral sources.

These very important sources of business are ones that nearly everyone neglects. Your friends, neighbors, acquaintances and others you meet at health clubs, civic organizations, or any other place are great sources of business. Tell everyone you come in contact with what you do for a living, that you are a mortgage banker and that you will be happy to assist them if they need to buy or refinance a home or investment property. Be sure you give them a few business cards, one for them and a couple to share. Mortgage banking is relationship sales. You sell yourself over a period of time based on relationships that you develop with Realtors, builders and everyone else you meet in your daily life. Take full advantage of those associations and relationships and let everyone know what you do, and that you can help them. Know too that you aren't exploiting your relationships but you are actually offering to help them in a very important way that also allows you to benefit from what you do for them.

People generally like to do business with friends and acquaintances so it is of upmost importance that you build a broad network of individuals who can be a resource for your mortgage banking practice. Get to know a lot of people. And, be absolutely certain that everyone you meet knows that you are a mortgage banker. Be sure to give them not just one business card, but two or three cards. Tell them that if one of their friends or colleagues needs financing to be certain to have them call you as you will take very good care of them. Whatever you do, don't use the phrase that you will give them a special "deal." The word "deal" makes it sound like you need to go out to the back alley to work out the details. Semantics are very important in constructing your image as a high level professional mortgage banker.

One cautionary note with regard to providing financing for close friends: sometimes people you know will be reluctant to have you handle their mortgage financing because they don't want their friends to know their personal financial matters. This is understandable, but by broaching this issue early you can avoid losing business to a competitor. I have used a statement like the following while having a casual conversation with friends to head off this type of situation in advance: "If you ever need mortgage financing, please let me help. No one will look out for you like I will and your personal financial information is totally confidential. Besides, aren't friends supposed to look out for friends?"

You may want to devise your own statement with several variations to use with friends, but it is important that you address it because otherwise you will lose business. To avoid that, you need to lay the foundation in advance. By devising a statement in advance to use when talking with your friends and acquaintances, you are more likely to present it in a smoother, more casual manner, making it sound less like a sales pitch and more of a genuine offer of friendship and assistance. Many of my closest friends were once clients; some were clients first and others, friends first. Since no one will look out for your friends as well as you, be certain they know that in advance. Besides, now that you have addressed this issue with them, they will feel guilty if they use a competitor for financing.

With people you know, you can take more of a counseling approach than a sales approach. Once these people know that you are a mortgage banker, they are much more likely to rely on you for mortgage services than go to another lender, but only if you have laid the foundation. Building a rapport with your friends and being their financial confidant will help you build your mortgage banking practice because it further augments your image as the expert that people can rely upon for competent advice.

It also serves to reduce the resistance that friends and relatives may have to doing business with you because of the need for them to disclose personal financial information. It provides the opportunity for them to more slowly reveal their finances so that they remain in their comfort zone. It allows you to build on the relationship rather than put it at risk by delving too quickly into an area where they are uncomfortable.

A perfect place to begin the conversation is with regard to the tax impact of a mortgage. Borrowers and real estate agents often think in terms of the tax deductibility of mortgage interest and taxes. However, people often misunderstand how the tax deductions work. Everyone needs to understand that if someone is in a 30% tax bracket then only 30% of the interest and taxes that they pay will ultimately be a direct deduction from their taxable income. That means that 70% of what they pay is not deductible or beneficial in any way other than to provide them with a place to live, which in itself can be very important.

Of course 100% of the interest and tax expense that the homeowner pays goes on the tax return but it is then reduced by "IRS math" to an amount equal to the taxpayer's tax rate. Buying a home and paying a mortgage is much more beneficial than paying rent, but having no mortgage payment is almost always best. Counsel your clients to think in terms of early payment of their mortgage unless they plan to be in the home for only a few years. Should they need to tap the equity in their home, there will be more of it. Then you can provide the equity loan.

It is not unheard of for a borrower to walk into your office to refinance their free and clear home for what they perceive to be the tax benefit of a mortgage. All they are going to do is end up paying refinance cost plus a lot of interest over many years and only a fraction of their expenditure will offer any tax benefit. Of course they can benefit in other ways from the cash they extract from the property, and if they are over age 62 they may be a candidate for a reverse mortgage to supplement their retirement income. Consider all the options.

This is an opportunity for you to either make a quick buck or more desirably, to display your integrity by explaining the tax aspects of mortgage interest. This will establish you as someone who people can rely upon for competent, honest advice. When meeting with this type of client, be certain to ask if they have an advisor such as an accountant, attorney or financial planner upon whom they rely. If so, with the client's permission, send the advisor a nice letter briefly explaining your meeting with your mutual client and the nature of your advice. You can then suggest to the advisor that since they may have greater knowledge of your mutual clients personal financial and business interest that they may want to review your recommendations with the client in the event there is information that was not shared with you that could impact the client's finances. Also be certain to mention to the advisor that you will be very happy to discuss with them the client's situation and the available options.

An important caveat: only send this letter if you advised the client not to refinance. If you are refinancing a property for them, wait until the loan has disbursed before sending a similar letter explaining what you did for the client. Since we can assume that you provided competent advice, offered the best possible loan product and acted in the client's best interest there is no need to alert their advisor until the transaction is complete. You don't want the advisor stepping in and improperly advising the client not to complete the financing or referring their client to another mortgage banker. Assuming that you acted in the best interest of the client, a letter after the transaction offers the potential for referrals. Put the advisor on your referral list for continuing follow up.

Every place you go and everyone you meet present an opportunity to be introduced to someone who is considering the purchase or refinance of real estate. Even those who are not personally considering such a transaction probably have a friend, acquaintance, family member or professional colleague who has mentioned that they are considering such a transaction. Fortunately for them, you can help.

It is important that you at least casually mention to everyone whom you meet that you are a mortgage banker. In fact, it is important that you develop several very short phrases much like when you broach the subject of helping your family and friends. You need several statements to that effect because you will often be "working a room" at a business or social event and you don't want people to overhear you using the same phrase over and over.

An easy way to introduce yourself and inject your profession is to ask other people that you meet what kind of work they do. Even if they don't reciprocate by asking what you do, you can simply inject that "I'm a mortgage banker with XYZ Mortgage Company." Always, always, always give each person you meet two or three of your business cards and tell them if they ever need help with mortgage financing that you will be very happy to assist them and that they may feel free to have their friends or colleagues call you if they need assistance with a mortgage or simply have a related question. Business cards should be shared liberally as they are not only the least expensive marketing tool that you have, but they are something that the recipient is very likely to keep for a long time. If you question the longevity of business cards, just check your desk drawer to see how many business cards from other people that you have kept.

You don't have to make a sales pitch to the people that you meet; you simply need to let them know what you do and be certain they have a couple of your business cards and if possible that you have their card. There is no guarantee that they will call you next week for financing or that they will ever call you. However, there is a far greater chance that they will call you if they know you are in the mortgage business and they have your business card with your contact information. They are also far more likely to share one of your business cards with someone else who may be looking for mortgage financing. It is all about building a network of relationships.

When you get involved with civic groups or other volunteer organizations, always give the people you meet one of your business cards as a means of providing them with your contact information. Since you will probably have a cell phone number on the card, you can simply say, "Here is my cell phone number." It will not look like you are promoting your mortgage banking business, but that you are simply offering a phone number so they can reach you. But, from the information on your business card they will probably notice that you are a mortgage banker. That may come in handy some day when they need to buy a home or refinance their current property or they hear someone else mention that they may need financing. Remember, you are not only a mortgage banker but a trusted member of the same organization.

Build your personal network by joining a civic club, such as Rotary or Kiwanis, and other community organizations such as the PTA / PTO at your children's school. If you belong to a health club, use that opportunity to network as well, but don't strike up a conversation in the showers - no pockets for business cards.

Mortgage bankers have it far easier than real estate agents, insurance agents and many others when networking, as people often feel that the real estate and insurance agents are trying to sell them something. An introduction to a mortgage banker often makes the individual feel that they now have an inside source that they can rely on for the best financing terms. How fortunate.

Real estate agents traditionally focus their marketing on a particular neighborhood, subdivision or a condominium project. They refer to this as "farming" because, much like the agribusiness for which it is named, there is a lot of cultivating before you get your "cash crop."

Real estate agents "farm" residential neighborhoods in an effort to get listings and generate sales from the people who live in the targeted community. This method can be equally as effective for the loan officer. Although some of the people will move out of the area and will have no use for your services, others will be refinancing, need an equity loan or are moving within the same town where you have the opportunity to finance the home they are buying. You get a double benefit if you farm a neighborhood where high producing real estate agents live because it gives you additional exposure to them.

Be certain you understand your market. Don't mail first time homebuyer literature to senior communities and don't send reverse mortgage or refinance information to rental communities.

Depending on the area where you work, the average time a homeowner lives in a house could run anywhere from three or four years to nine or ten years. Even at the slower turnover rate of every ten years, if you, as a mortgage loan officer, farm an area with one thousand homes, there will be one hundred homes that change hands every year. And, many of those who didn't move may need to refinance their first mortgage or obtain a second mortgage or home equity line of credit. Perhaps they are intent on living out their retirement in that community and could benefit from a reverse mortgage. If you farm an area, consider one with about a thousand homes or several smaller areas totaling about a thousand homes. Mail a large postcard (5½" x 8½" is a good size) to each resident about every six weeks. If you mail to 1/6th of the residents each week, that is about 167 postcards per week for a subdivision of about one thousand homes. Consistency is the key to success. It will take approximately seven mailings or nearly a year before you are the recognized mortgage banker for that area.

If you regularly drive through the neighborhood you have selected to farm, as well as watching the homes for sale section of the local newspaper, you can identify those homeowners who are trying to sell their homes themselves. These people are known in the real estate community by the acronym FSBO (For Sale By Owner) which is pronounced "fizbo."

You can assist the FSBO homeowner by providing them with a "property information" form that they can hand out to prospective buyers. These forms can include the homeowner's property information and photos. They can describe several financing options, the amount of down payment and closing costs that will be necessary to purchase the property as well as the monthly payment that will correspond with each of several down payment amounts at current interest rates. Do not however, list the actual interest rate, unless your sample rate is slightly lower than the market rate as borrowers will use that to shop around for better rates. Of course, if you state a rate you must also include the APR. And, don't forget, by law, if you advertise some financing terms you must disclose all of the financing terms.

The property information forms can also indicate the amount of income that the borrower is likely to need to qualify for the financing. If the homeowner gives one of these forms to each prospective buyer then the homeowner becomes a marketing agent for you because each form should prominently display your name, contact information and your very attractive photo. One additional and very significant benefit to you is that every FSBO will be inundated with real estate agents trying to get the listing. Each agent is very likely to pick up one of your "property information" forms. Once again, marketing from which you can benefit.

Once you have developed the relationship with the homeowner, you are in a good position to discuss with them why they should consider using a real estate firm to sell their home. If you are successful, you can help the homeowner by referring them to an agent with whom you currently have a business relationship or one with whom you would like to do business. This provides an exceptional opportunity to "lock in" a relationship with a real estate agent.

When the opportunity exists to make the referral, be sure you let the sales agent know that you are referring it to them because of the previous borrowers they have referred to you or to provide an opportunity for you and the agent to work together (for the first time). Be certain in either instance that you make it very clear that you expect to handle the financing on this property, or if circumstances don't allow it, that they will refer the buyer of another property to you instead. Also point out that real estate agents make much more on each transaction than loan officers so that the pay back should not be a one-for-one arrangement but more like three or four referrals from the agent to each one you refer to them.

You will often have greater success in gaining access to FSBO's than real estate agents, because your services do not cost the homeowner anything, where the services of a real estate agent may be presumed to cost them six or seven percent. However, statistics indicate that real estate agents can generally get a higher price for the property than the owner who attempts to sell without the assistance of a broker. The actual net difference is close to one percent. For a mere one percent, the services of a competent real estate agent are a real bargain. And, if the real estate agent happens to charge a brokerage fee of 5% or less, then the real estate services are effectively free to the homeowner.

Many referral sources can be cultivated through the use of a regular mailing or even email and an occasional telephone call. Over time you should make an effort to meet them personally. Always keep in mind that it is the personal relationships that drive the business. Mailings and phone calls are excellent for keeping your name and some pertinent information in front of good referral sources, but you cannot expect to receive any actual referrals until they have had an opportunity to meet you in person.

An additional source of business is the renter who may be a candidate to purchase a home. To develop this source of business, you need to locate several apartment complexes that have relatively high rents that would correspond with the proposed mortgage payment of homes for sale in your area or in a nearby community.

In order to determine which of these renters may be interested in purchasing a home, send a letter or colorful postcard to every tenant in each complex (one complex at a time) inviting them to "stop paying the landlord and start paying themselves by investing in a home of their own." Include pictures of homes in the area that are currently for sale and that are in the price range of what the renter should be able to buy based on what they pay in rent. The pictures should be obtained from a real estate agent and should be of properties they currently have listed for sale or properties listed by other agents in their office and used with the agent's permission. Most agents will jump at the chance to have their listings promoted as they can show the postcard to the homeowner as evidence of how hard they are working to sell the property.

Include in the letter an invitation to attend a "Home Buyers Seminar." The seminar should be held near the apartment complex so that it is convenient for the tenants to attend. In some cases you may even be able to rent a meeting room at the apartment complex. However, the management may not allow you to use the facilities if they understand your purpose. If that is the case, check local hotels, civic association meeting places or even public libraries. Often a meeting room at a library will be available free of charge if you don't charge for the seminar.

If your office is in the area you may hold the seminar there or if you are associated with a bank with a branch in the vicinity, you may arrange with the branch manager to hold the seminar in the bank's lobby after closing hours in the evening or on a Saturday afternoon. A seminar not only provides an opportunity for you to generate new business but it brings potential new depositors and borrowers to the bank.

You should require reservations for the seminar so that you can plan for the number of people who will attend. The maximum number of people attending should be ten to fifteen people, because you want to have time to talk personally with as many people as possible after the presentation. Because everyone who makes a reservation will not show up, accept up to twenty reservations. If you have more requests for reservations, simply offer to schedule another seminar the following week or offer a personal conference at your office. You can even hold a seminar at their home if they invite their friends or neighbors who are also interested in buying a home. Even if you only get two or three people to register for a seminar, hold it anyway, just set up the room for a more intimate gathering. This isn't as efficient as starting with a larger number and eliminating those who aren't actual prospects, but it may still generate some transactions.

Most loan officers conduct homebuyer seminars with a real estate agent, an accountant or a home inspector. If you should choose to do so, the seminar should consist of three presentations of about ten minutes each. First on the list should be the real estate agent with whom you have worked. It should be one who you feel is very capable and competent and who will make a good impression on the attendees. Logically, this should be the same agent who provided you with photographs of properties in the area for your marketing material.

Real estate agents should talk briefly about how to go about selecting a home and what to look for in terms of area, potential resale, or buying a smaller home and grow with it. They should also consider issues regarding the condition of the home and using home inspection services, etc. The next speaker could be an accountant who can present the financial benefits of home ownership and give an example of the effect the mortgage interest deduction would have on someone in the estimated income range of the prospects in attendance. Again, the speaker should be someone who will give a good presentation and who will instill confidence in the people attending the seminar. Alternately, you can have a home inspector make a presentation rather than the real estate agent or the accountant. The real estate agent, accountant or home inspector should be happy to take part in the presentation because of the opportunity to generate business from those in attendance.

Your presentation should cover the various loan types, FHA, VA and conventional financing and the down payment requirements that each would require. You can give an example of a house of a value typical in your market area, or at least compatible with the estimated earnings of those in the seminar, and tell how much down payment they would need in each case, what the monthly payment would be, and the annual income and maximum debts they would need to qualify.

Be certain to tell each participant that you and the other speakers would be very happy to talk with them after the seminar to discuss their particular situation. Also include on their registration form (yes, you absolutely need a registration form) an area for them to request additional information or ask a specific question. Have someone from your office attend the seminar with you. They can stand at the door when the seminar is over to be sure that everyone's registration form is collected.

Now that I have explained how to include a real estate agent, my recommendation is that you not include an agent. You may consider including a home inspector instead. The reason is very simple. To the consumer, the banker (that would be you) has far greater credibility than a real estate agent. Prospective buyers/borrowers will avoid a seminar if they think they may be collared by a real estate agent. At the appropriate time following a seminar you can and should refer these prospective buyers to a competent real estate agent with whom you do business. When you refer the buyer to the agent, there is greater credibility for the agent than when the agent is at the seminar and the buyer feels they have been forced to accept that agent. You will also note that after you meet with the prospective borrowers, you might feel it is appropriate to refer them to different agents. Keep in mind that you are working for long-term relationships, not one-time transactions and that everyone benefits if the borrower is referred to an agent that is a good match for them.

Out of a group of ten to fifteen people, you will typically get three to five borrowers. If you present one seminar per month, that will be three to five additional loans per month over a period of time. You cannot depend on this as your only source of business but it will add up to a very substantial supplement to your business.

Chapter 21
Professional Practitioner Referrals

Although the number of mortgage referrals will probably be substantially lower from professional practitioners, such as attorneys, accountants, financial planners and similar professional sources they often represent higher quality business. The clients of these referral sources usually consist of individuals in an upper income bracket which allows them to retain these professionals. It also means that they may be buying or refinancing more expensive property with a larger mortgage loan.

Because clients place a higher level of confidence in their attorney than their real estate agent, for example, the attorney's referral carries a greater degree of weight. This is due in part to attorneys having longer relationships with their clients, while relationships with the real estate agents tend to be on an "as needed" basis without loyalty to any particular agent. The high regard the client has for the attorney transfers to people recommended by the attorney. Therefore, an attorney recommendation places the mortgage banker who was the recipient of the referral in a higher position compared with his or her peers. The same holds true of referrals from other professional referral sources. Consider the following potential business sources:

Small banks & credit unions - Small financial institutions with no residential mortgage department can be a great conduit for business. They will be happy to have a mortgage financing option to offer to their depositors, especially if you are with an independent mortgage banker rather than a depository institution competing with them in the same market. Smaller institutions tend to have closer, more trusting relationships with their depositors. When you are the loan officer they recommend to assist with a mortgage loan, that reference carries a lot of weight and you are afforded a great deal of credibility. You might even ask the bank if they would like to fund and hold the loan once it is processed if this is satisfactory with your employer. This effectively gives the financial institution an adjunct mortgage department to handle loans for their depositors with no overhead expense. It also may provide you with an alternative investor for other loans that are not available through your company.

Attorneys – Attorneys are always a source of quality business but divorce attorneys can be a particularly fertile resource as their clients are typically going through a divorce and many will sell a house to settle their marital financial matters with their spouse. Thereafter, they may buy another home. At that point both parties to a divorce are not only candidates for a mortgage loan but are also prospects that you can refer to a real estate agent to help them sell the current home and buy a new home. If the mortgage banker and the real estate agent are particularly nimble they can help both parties to the divorce, but at great risk of getting caught in the crossfire.

Financial Planners – Most financial planners make their money by selling insurance and securities. They often find that their clients are better able to purchase the products they sell, when the clients refinance or consolidate debt to lower their monthly payments or take cash out of a property so they can free-up some funds to buy the financial planner's investment products. Of course, many financial planners are truly looking only at the benefit to the client of buying another home or refinancing for better rate or terms. Just be certain that you understand which financial planners earn income from commissions from the sale of financial products and those that charge a fee for developing a personal financial plan and offering advice to their clients and receive no commission. Also, be aware of Securities and Exchange Commission rules that restrict borrowing money for investments.

Accountants – Generally, accountants are looking at cash flow issues, typically for individuals and for small businesses. Consequently, most of their referrals are related to refinance transactions for improved cash flow. If you can offer both residential and commercial mortgages that will give you the flexibility to handle all their clients. You don't need to personally handle the commercial loans as long as there is someone in your company who can do that and share the fee with you of course. Remember, you are not a charitable entity; always get part of any fees that are charged, as long as there are no legal restrictions prohibiting the sharing of fees between lenders or loan officers.

Certified Public Accountants – The CPA's primary objective is often tax driven. You need to be conversant with most of the major tax implications to talk intelligently with the CPA. Naturally, you can acquiesce to their expertise and let them teach you what you need to know. Just be certain that you start with some basic tax knowledge and use the CPA to build your tax expertise.

Always remember that it is not only the clients of the professional financial planners, attorneys, accountants, CPA's, etc. that are prospective business clients, but the professionals themselves. For this reason it may be very beneficial to offer each of them a "professional courtesy discount" on fees should they obtain financing through you for themselves. A discount of $500 is usually appropriate and is available only to the referral source and not to their clients. If you would like to offer another discount of, say $250 for their clients as a benefit for them utilizing the professional referral source that is your choice. However, such a benefit runs the risk of sounding as though you are buying the business and that the prospective borrower may be getting inferior service if the mortgage banker needs to "pay for" the business with an inducement. The discount to the referral source is different because it is in appreciation of the relationship they have with you and the business they send your way and an acknowledgement that you are both at the same professional level, just serving different business segments for the same clientele. Cultivating professional business sources may take time and finesse, but like other parts of your mortgage banking practice, it is a long term investment in your career.

So, now you have a list of some of the professions and business that can benefit from your services. How do you find them? The Yellow Pages of the phone book are really an excellent place to start. Another resource for those who are licensed by the state is the state agency responsible for their licensure. Information on most licensed professionals is available from the state as public information.

Since you have naturally included all the prospective professional business referral sources you located in the Yellow Pages and elsewhere into your master database, you can now send each of them an introductory letter that runs no more than half of one page including a sentence that you would like to meet them briefly just to introduce yourself. Mention that you will give them a call to arrange a convenient time to stop by. Also, include a sentence to the effect that if you can be of assistance to them in the interim, to give you a call. Obviously, include your phone number. Enclose a copy of your "Mortgage Banker" brochure along with two or three business cards. Be sure to call them the following week to set up a time to get together. If they decline your offer to get together simply tell them that you understand that they are very busy and that you will keep in touch in the event you can be of assistance to their clients. That evening, write a short handwritten note telling them that it was good talking with them and that you look forward to helping them or their clients with any mortgage finance matter. If you get an appointment, keep it brief; maybe ten minutes. You don't want to take too much of their time or you own. After all, you are both busy with other business commitments.

Realistically, you will get appointments with about one in six or seven professionals that you call. The important thing is that you make contact with them and that you keep in touch through regular notes, letters, brochures, etc. so that they start developing a sense of a business connection with you. About every six months, call them again and be certain to ask if they ever have situations where their clients need mortgage financing. Whether their answer is yes, or no, ask to whom they would refer their clients. Be sure you tell them that you provide high level mortgage banking services similar to what their clients would receive in a financial institution's private banking department, just at much lower cost. Tell them that the quality of the service you offer will reflect well on them and that you will appreciate any clients that they refer to you. Reiterate that if they need mortgage financing for themselves that you do offer a $500 professional courtesy discount toward their closing costs. Tell them that it was good talking with them and that you will keep in touch. As in all referral contacts, if possible, inject some personal matters into the conversation, both about them and about you. Remember, you are trying to build a business relationship. Each call should not take more than five to seven minutes.

Because of the cost of marketing to each professional segment, you might want to initially focus on just one group, such as lawyers or financial planners. As you build your clientele you can expand to other professional groups. It is more important that you market yourself competently. If you are spreading yourself too thin with regard to your time or if your budget is too limited to do a really good marketing job, then limit yourself to one or two groups for which you can afford both the time and money to cultivate their referral business.

Your focus should always be on quality not quantity. If you market yourself well to a small group, you will receive business referrals from them, affording you the opportunity to spend a little more money to market to a larger group until you have reached that point where you simply don't have the time to market to more people. Like all sales, you start with little money but lots of time and ultimately build your business until you have much more money but less time for new clients. Of course, at that point, hire one or more assistants and assign most of the behind the scenes work to them so that you are exclusively the rain maker for your mortgage banking practice.

Chapter 22
Business from Retail Merchants

Mortgage bankers often neglect retailers as a source of mortgage referrals, but they can be a very fertile business conduit. Naturally you need to focus on retailers that sell high dollar products since those are the ones that require the customer to pay a lot of cash, take on a large consumer loan, or more reasonably, obtain a tax-advantaged home equity loan, line of credit or refinance their property, taking out enough cash to complete the transaction.

Consider each of the following retail businesses and think about how you can help each of them increase sales by providing financing that is more beneficial to their customers:

Home renovation contractors

Automobile dealers

Motor home and travel trailer retailers

Boat dealers

Furniture stores

Billiard and pool table retailers

Paving contractors

Swimming pool contractors

Heating and air conditioning contractors

Most of these retail businesses have never done business with a mortgage banker and many have probably never been approached by a mortgage banker for business referrals. For those reasons, it is best to approach each business personally rather than beginning with the usual introductory letter because the opportunity to "bond" with them is much better in a face-to-face meeting than what a letter or phone call might offer. It is much easier to explain how they can benefit by referring their customers to you when you are there in person. Unlike many of the professional referral sources and the real estate related businesses, referring customers to a mortgage banker for financing may be a new concept. A concept, that once explained, will make a great deal of sense to them.

Since most consumers buy homes, automobiles, furniture and virtually every other product based on "how much down and how much per month," you can make your case for retail merchants, referring their customers to you. Because mortgage financing offers a longer payment term and lower interest rates, resulting in lower monthly payments than typical consumer financing, their prospective customer can buy more products or the more expensive model and still have a lower monthly payment than typical consumer financing will allow. It may also mean that their customer can now afford to buy the product that was too expensive with typical consumer financing.

The biggest challenge will be the retailer's desire for instant financing. They want to take advantage of the customer's impulse purchase. In most cases their buyers can get instant approval for consumer financing through any of several finance companies. Usually the customer and the retailer do not want to wait for the customer's home to be appraised and the loan to close, and of course, the three day right of rescission. No problem.

You can simply arrange with the retailer to provide you with the name, address and phone number of every customer to whom they have sold a product as well as those who did not buy or may still be contemplating the purchase. In most cases your financing will be after the sale has taken place as a way to improve the financing terms for the consumer by reducing their interest rate and monthly payment. Naturally you have the opportunity to help them consolidate some of their other obligations into a single loan with one monthly payment that should be substantially lower than what they may already be paying.

In many retail environments the business and the sales agent benefit financially if the buyer uses their consumer financing source. Because the remuneration to the retailer is impacted by such an arrangement, the fact that mortgage financing takes longer actually works to everyone's benefit. The consumer can make an immediate purchase using the consumer financing; the sales agent makes a sale and receives both the sales commission and the consumer finance incentive fee. The consumer obtains the mortgage financing after the purchase for better terms and pays off the consumer loan. Then, you get paid on the mortgage loan.

Sometimes homeowners will say that they don't want to put a mortgage on their home to buy furniture or a car or a motor home, etc. What you need to point out is that they are paying the same price and acquiring the same amount of debt regardless of the type of loan. The big difference is that mortgage loans generally carry a lower interest rate that is tax deductible and, because it can be repaid over a longer period of time, the payments may be substantially lower. You are just offering them an opportunity for a lower monthly payment and a lower interest rate with tax savings. The longer term and lower monthly payments gives the borrower more flexibility because they can always pre-pay the loan or make the minimum monthly payment if their cash flow is tight rather than be locked into a high monthly payment on a consumer loan.

Ask every retailer to let you put a "take one" stand in their showroom. You can create an attractive brochure with a quick comparison of consumer financing rates, terms and payments with those offered by a few mortgage financing options that you offer. A more expensive version of the "take one" brochures can have a detachable postage paid return postcard for the retail customer to fill out and mail back to you requesting information on mortgage financing. Be certain the card has space for their telephone number and address. As financial markets move and rates change, you will need to update your brochures. The brochures should always be imprinted with the date the rates are effective. Be certain to check with the retailer regularly to be sure they have enough brochures available for customers. This is a good task for Saturday when you may have a more flexible schedule and there is a greater opportunity for you to be in the store when the customers are there.

The manner in which you contact the retail customer can vary between simply mailing a letter and brochure or a telephone call. The phone call is far more effective. However, because of the "Do Not Call" laws, you need to be absolutely certain that the number that you are calling is not listed on the Do Not Call Registry. Your company may maintain a current copy of the Do Not Call

Database. However, as the list must be updated monthly, it is very expensive to maintain and usually only the larger mortgage lenders incur that expense. Even then, it is usually used only as part of a telemarketing department and not available to retail loan officer. However, it does not cost you anything to inquire of your management if the list is available. If you don't have access to the Do Not Call list then you need to limit the marketing to the retailer's customers to mail, although a return postcard provided with your letter can obtain the customer's permission for you to call. Of course, the retailer can also obtained written permission from the customer that will allow you to call them.

Remember that virtually every retail business is a prospective referral source. While those that sell high price products and services are the most viable sources of business, it never hurts to have your "take one" displays in every retail store in town. Just remember that you need to service the accounts by refilling the dispensers regularly. Not only will you get inquiries from your brochures, but you will develop good relationships with the merchants who can refer their customers, friends and everyone with whom they come in contact as well as using your mortgage services themselves. You will be building a strong, diversified network.

Here are some retail merchants that you might contact and the benefit that you can offer to each:

Renovation Contractors – Borrower may refinance or obtain a second mortgage or line of credit to cover the cost of renovating their home. Most of the second mortgages will be small but there will also be some substantial refinance loans. Many loan officers earn very good income from second mortgages and lines of credit depending on the compensation plan with their employer.

Auto Dealers – Buyers of both new and used vehicles may enjoy lower rates and tax benefits by financing a vehicle purchase with a home equity loan rather than with dealer-provided financing. Just remember that most auto agencies want to arrange the financing because they make money by brokering car loan to the finance company. But there is no reason you can't close on a mortgage loan a couple days after they close on the dealer provided loan and take possession of the vehicle. The benefit of doing it this way is that the dealer and auto salesperson are happy because they get an immediate sale plus their override on the auto loan. There is no delay to the borrower while they wait for their second mortgage or equity line of credit to be processed, the property appraised, loan approved, closed and funded. Remember there is a three day right of rescission so the total time with equity loans is usually longer than the borrower and the dealer want to wait to deliver the new car. Of course, the borrower needs to have sufficient equity in their home to finance the purchase of a vehicle in this manner.

Motor Homes and Travel Trailer Dealers – These puppies can be very expensive, sometimes more than a traditional home. As long as the buyer has real estate of sufficient value and enough equity, you can usually provide more attractive financing by refinancing their home or providing a second mortgage to provide the money to purchase their recreational vehicles.

Furniture and Pool Table Retailers – Second mortgages and lines of credit generally have lower rates and longer terms than retail financing, which means lower monthly payments. Explain to the dealer that they can sell more products or higher priced products with larger profit margins if they help the buyer keep their payment low by using a mortgage loan.

Swimming Pool Contractors - Help them sell a swimming pool by providing the homeowner with the financing. You can even help the contractor generate business by sharing the cost of a joint marketing campaign. Mail a postcard to homeowners suggesting that they can have a new swimming pool for their summer enjoyment paid for with the equity in their home. Let their home pay for its own improvements.

Paving Contractors – When a homeowner chooses to pave or re-pave a driveway, it can be very expensive. You can help.

Heating and Air Conditioning Contractors - When it is time to replace or upgrade the HVAC system in a customer's home, the cost can be daunting. Low rate, long-term mortgage financing may be just the answer and allow the contractor to enhance the homeowner's HVAC system with an air filtration system, a humidifier or a dehumidifier. Because newer high efficiency HVAC systems will probably reduce the customer's utility bill, the savings from a more efficient system could offset much of the monthly payment on the new mortgage loan used to acquire the system. This means a higher dollar sale and more profit for the contractor. Here again is an opportunity for joint marketing with a contractor.

Boat Dealers – Despite the old saying that a boat is a hole in the water into which you throw money, they are a luxury that many people enjoy. Set up a booth at the next boat show and explain to boat dealers, as well as prospective boat buyers, how you can help them if the boat customer has sufficient equity in their home.

Business Owners – Although every business does not survive the initial years and many that do create only a marginal income for the owner, there are many businesses that have survived, matured and prospered providing their owners with above average incomes. For many who are in this category, the additional income presents a need for appropriate investment options. Real estate investment is a viable way for business owners and many other high income individuals to diversify their investment portfolio. The leverage available through mortgage financing allows an investor to multiply their return on investment property. Consider all the business owners or highly compensated employees that you may be able to assist. They may include the owner of the local dry cleaning shop, physicians, lawyers, wholesaler, stock brokers and the owners of virtually every other business in town.

The number and type of retailers and professional practitioners that are both referral sources and potential clients themselves is limited only by your energy, enthusiasm and imagination. Everyone is a prospect until proven otherwise.

Chapter 23
Internet Marketing

The Internet has become an integral part of every business operation and mortgage banking is clearly no exception. Most mortgage institutions maintain an Internet presence but not all offer an on-line mortgage loan application. Even those that provide an Internet portal for consumers to submit mortgage applications often do not provide direct access for the clients to submit applications to individual mortgage loan officers. The rationale is rather simple, but equally flawed; mortgage lenders are afraid that an application that goes directly to the loan officer and bypasses the company's normal on-line application system might fall into the great Internet abyss.

Because there are regulatory criteria for responding to a prospective borrower's application, lenders are afraid that if a loan officer is on vacation, out sick or has left the company, that the application will not be acknowledged within the required time limits, putting the company at risk of violating compliance regulations. This is a valid concern, but one that can be mitigated.

Most mortgage lenders that offer the convenience of an Internet application direct the applications to their company's central mortgage loan processing center, where the applications are processed and closed without the loan officer being aware that the borrower has applied for a loan. Of course the loan officer doesn't get paid for the loan either. This arrangement forces loan officers to steer prospective applicants away from the company's official website; sometimes to their own "pirate" site. These loan officer "pirate" sites may resemble the company's official site, but the applications go directly to the loan officer rather than through the company's official application portal, creating the potential for compliance challenges that the company wants to avoid.

The ideal on-line application systems allow the loan officer's clients to submit an application through a website that is dedicated to that specific loan officer. The application goes directly to the loan officer and for compliance purposes, a copy of the application will go to a central monitoring center to be certain that a proper and timely response is made to the application. This allows the loan officer to put a web address on all their marketing pieces to encourage on-line applications which allows the loan officer to not only monitor the loan processing but most importantly to receive production credit, and of course, to be paid for that loan.

Without on-line capability, most loan officers have to consider moving to another mortgage company with more robust technology, including on-line application capability or becoming an independent mortgage broker. Otherwise, they will continue to struggle with an antiquated system that limits their production capability.

Since we can't cause the large companies to change their technology, I will focus on what the independent mortgage broker or lender may do to enhance their web presence.

For an independent mortgage broker or lender and their loan officers to have an on-line application, they can create or buy an application package from a company that provides mortgage loan processing systems (LPS). Most packages come with an Internet based application system, either as a standard feature or as an option that will comply with all regulatory criteria, while delivering an applicant's loan application directly to the designated recipient. There are also companies that produce stand-alone application system that can be integrated into the lender's website. These systems generally have the capability to load each on-line application directly into the lender's LPS.

The first step in establishing an Internet presence is to get a domain name that is simple and appropriate for your mortgage lending practice (www.xyzmortgage.com). Of course you need to have a website at that location to receive your visitors and a mortgage loan application page where prospective borrowers can apply for a loan or get pre-approved. This domain is what we might call your primary domain. This is the web address that referrals who know you are likely to use to apply on line for their mortgage.

Most people look for a unique and appropriate domain name, such as the company name, or a variation of that name. However, research shows that only two percent (2%) of Internet web pages are accessed by the user directly inputting a specific web address. The other 98% use a search engine, such as Google, Lycos, Bing, AltaVista, Yahoo, etc., and typing in a few words that describe what they are looking for.

Your "primary" domain is great for the two percent who know who you are and look for you by name, but there is also a lot of business from people looking for a mortgage who have absolutely no idea who you are. How can you help these people find you? You can use multiple "secondary" domains.

When you are considering domain names for your "secondary" websites, you need to step back and think like the customer. When search engines display the results, they have a protocol that matches the key words input by the person making the search with websites on the Internet. The search engines parse the information prioritizing in the following order: domain name, web page title and then descriptive "key words" that appear on the web page.

What this means is that a domain name of "www.xyzmortgage.com" is very unlikely to be pulled up on a search engine; at least not near the top of the list displayed. In fact a recent search on Google for the word "mortgage" produced 142 million responses. Even if you are in the middle of the pack, listed at number 71 million, it isn't going to do you much good. If you are not on one of the first three pages you are very unlikely to have anyone even find your website from a search engine inquiry. In fact, you really need to be on the very first page and the closer to the top you are, the more likely that you will actually get a "hit" on your website as a result.

Of course, there is a more certain way to end up at the top of the first page of each search engine and that is to have a sponsored site. This means that you pay the search engine for the privilege of being near the top of the first page of search results. If you are considering this option, check with the various search engines to see what the cost may be. One hint: it is very expensive.

If you actually get someone to your website, does that mean you will get a loan application? Of course not; in fact the average Internet conversion rate is only 1%. You have to get 100 people to

170

your website just to get one application. And the average website gets only ten visitors per day. Considering how many people visit the major websites such as Amazon.com and CNN.com each day, you have to recognize that 80% of all websites get no visitors at all.

When you are selecting your "secondary" domain names, don't be concerned about keeping them short or having your company name included. Use words the borrower might use when looking for a lender. If you are uncertain, open a search engine page and put in the words a borrower might use when looking for a mortgage lender. Then you might check with one of the domain registrars to see if some of those word combinations are available as domain names. Remember, these domains are to drive traffic to your mortgage application page so their mission is to consist of words that will show up high in the search engine results. If you find a great combination but it is not available as a ".com" domain, then take the ".net" or the next available web "extension." Although the ".com" is the most popular domain extension and the one that will get listed on the search engines ahead of other extensions, it is still beneficial to take a subservient extension if the domain name itself is likely to score well on the search engines.

You have a couple of options regarding the use of multiple domain names. The first of course is to have multiple websites all with the exactly the same content. The second choice is to have all the secondary domains "redirect" to your primary site. Experts tell us that multiple sites are best because virus protection software will often stop a redirect to another site and require the consumer to manually approve the transfer to the primary site. The problem is that the consumer doesn't know what is at the primary site nor do they understand why the virus software is requiring them to manually authorize the redirect to the primary site. In most cases the consumer will simply abandon the site and go back to the search engine to find another mortgage provider that doesn't present the perceived risk of your site. Therefore, multiple sites are best.

So, what domain names should you look for? Naturally you need a primary domain that reflects, as closely as possible, the name of your company or the individual name of the loan officer. For your secondary websites, domain names simply need to reflect those words that prospective borrowers may insert in the search window. They can be very descriptive such as: www.MortgageArizonaPhoenixLowInterestRates.com, or any other combination of words that describe what you offer or what you believe prospective borrowers may use to find a mortgage lender. There are websites that can help you determine which key words are used most often by Internet searchers. To find them, simply type "key words" in your favorite search engine.

You can add additional key words in your website's HTML code or insert the words near the top of your websites that may appear in a search engine inquiry. If you don't want the words to appear on your website, just make the font color of the words the same as the background color on that part of your website. That way you can simply insert a string of words without worrying about them appearing in a relevant format. But, be careful as the words may appear in the search engines displayed results even though they are not visible on the website.

The more closely the borrower's search terms match your domain name or other key words in your web page, the more likely you are to appear near the top of the search engine results. It doesn't matter that the domain name is really strange or long or that it is an ".info" rather than a ".com" (although .com is best). The objective is to have a domain name that closely matches what someone searching for a mortgage is likely to put in the search engine.

This now brings us to the Internet's younger cousins, the blog, social network sites such as Facebook and quick connections such as Twitter. The question here is how much time can you commit to these sites and how much benefit can you garner from these contacts? Of course some of these mechanisms for staying in contact with your referral sources may fade while new ones may emerge over time.

The age of your referral sources may be a clue to how beneficial these marketing avenues may be. Certainly younger sources and early adopters may embrace these links but the older sources may not. The other question is how can you use these to benefit your mortgage banking practice?

If you used these communications avenues, you must use them wisely. Don't send an email or tweet to announce that you have developed a strange new rash. Only use them in a professional manner to communicate business related information. For example, you can announce that the yield on the ten year bond has moved up or down and that mortgage rates are likely to follow. It doesn't take long to compose and send brief email or tweets but maintaining a blog can be time consuming and a Facebook account can have negative implications if your "friends" start posting negative comments about your service or rates. Or they post comments of a political or religious character that may offend people.

Websites are the safest venue since they are a one way communication from you to anyone who accesses your site. All they see is what you want them to see. Twitter and email are similar in that every recipient reads only what you want them to read. Blogs and social sites present some risks as most have the opportunity for other people to post their comments. Yes, you can usually delete any that you feel are inappropriate, but then you have to sit at your computer watching for something that may be offensive.

You will need to use your judgment as to which, if any of these venues that you use to communicate with your business sources. Just keep it highly professional.

Chapter 24
Advertising as a Business Development Tool

To complete your marketing effort you may consider purchasing adverting space in a variety of publications or even on local radio or cable television stations. Broadcast TV is simply too expensive for a loan officer to even consider.

The key to successful advertising is sufficient creativity to draw attention to the ad and consistency of regular placement. Advertising must catch the eye of the potential customer and it must be applied with consistency. If the ads are updated or otherwise changed, it is highly beneficial to adhere to the previous format so that consumers recognize you and your company. This allows you to utilize and leverage your previous advertising.

Most of the time, adverting is the purview of the large mortgage companies and seldom the domain of the individual loan officer. However, strategically placed and consistently run ads can keep your name in front of your referral sources and stimulate business from individual borrowers whom you have no other means of reaching. Even with people you already know, advertising adds a level of credibility because they see your name and picture in print.

Advertising can be used to drive traffic to your website where the prospective customer can use a program to determine the amount of financing for which they might qualify. Naturally, you should have a section where they can use an abbreviated mortgage application to get pre-approved to buy a property for which you should charge a small fee, maybe $25. This should cover your credit report cost. The investment of even $25 by an individual indicates that they are serious about being approved so that they can buy a property.   Naturally, you should have a full mortgage loan application for the borrower who is preparing to execute a contract to buy a property or currently owns a home they wish to refinance.

Websites are a wonderful tool, but they are useless if customers don't use them.   For that, the customer must be made aware that the website exists and be encouraged to use it for mortgage financing.   That requires advertising in strategic places on the Internet and in real estate magazines, community newspapers or regional magazines.   As our society has transitioned to the Internet as a friendly intermediary for conducting business, people are more willing to access a website than to pick up the telephone to call a mortgage lender.   The Internet gives them a sense of privacy and security because they can "play" with the site without initially divulging their identity.   It allows them to buy rather than being sold.

There is another source of advertising that may be free or very low cost.   If you can convince real estate agents to let you attach a rider to their real estate signs you can provide a phone number for buyers to call you for financing information.   This will keep your name in front of prospective customers and other real estate agents.   This may prove to be a low return form of advertising, but it is also very low cost so you have very little to lose.   The rider should be as brief as possible and limited to no more than three lines as more lines means smaller font which make the sign unreadable.

A sign rider should read something like this: Line #1 "Financing By" Line #2 "Joe Smith" or alternatively "xyz Mortgage" and Line #3 "800-555-1212."   You could even leave off your name as long as the phone number goes directly to you.

Having your name on the sign however tells other real estate agents that you are that agent's preferred lender. That has value to you even if you are paying for the privilege. You will always have the cost of having the signs painted and sometimes you will need to pay a "gratuity" to the real estate agent for the benefit of placing your sign on their listing.

When proposing the rider to the real estate agent, explain that it is an extra tool that they can use when making a listing presentation to a homeowner. The rider provides another way to generate inquiries from prospective buyers. People may like the house but are uncertain whether they can afford the home or qualify for the mortgage. They may be more comfortable addressing the financing with a lender before looking at the property. This is one more way to draw in a prospective buyer who may otherwise not realize that they can afford the home and qualify for the financing necessary to complete the purchase. It is one more way to attract a few more qualified buyers.

The other benefit to the real estate agent is that, while some inquiries that you may receive will be from prospective buyers who may not qualify for that particular home, they may qualify for another property in a different price range. After you have made this determination and pre-approved the buyer, you can then refer them back to the real estate agent who can sell them another house.

Chapter 25
Do You Need A Partner?

The long hours that a loan officer must invest in their career can sometimes be more demanding than you bargained for when you first entered the business. Those interrupted evenings and weekends can leave you with very little time for yourself or to be with your family and friends. Unfortunately, nearly all successful careers, be they in mortgage banking or in other professions, require the investment of a substantial amount of time.

One of the best ways to give yourself a break and maintain an excellent rapport with your customers is to develop a partnership with another loan officer or a mortgage loan processor in your firm. This does not need to be a formal partnership with written agreements, but a simple verbal arrangement will usually work just fine. But, if you feel a written agreement of your arrangement is appropriate, then by all means use one as it eliminates misunderstandings.

The purpose of a partnership is to give each of you some time to yourself to take a vacation or even an evening out to dinner without your cell phone interfering. It allows you to relax and know you will not be interrupted, while at the same time knowing that your clients will be taken care of and that you will not lose business because you were not available.

There are two cardinal rules that relate to this partnership arrangement: 1. the compensation agreement must be very clear if there is to be a sharing of fees, and 2. it is good to work out a schedule several weeks in advance so you can both plan your work and your personal activities.

How does the partnership work? If you are going out of town or even if you will be available but want some uninterrupted time to yourself or with your family, use call forwarding to redirect calls to your partner's cell phone so they can respond to your customers. Do not tell your real estate agents you will not be available, because if they know you will not personally respond when you are called, they will call one of the other loan officers they do business with. This is the whole purpose of the partnership, to create continuity to keep you from losing business while getting a break from the business. Even if you are going for a vacation of several weeks, your partner can simply state that you are out of town for a couple days and ask how they can help. By using a call forwarding system you never have to risk losing business. You can have the agents call your regular cell phone number with the calls going directly to your partner when you are not available.

Selecting a partner is a very important decision. Put yourself in the position of the real estate agent and ask if you would want to do business with this loan officer or processor. Are they knowledgeable and reliable? Do they have a congenial personality that will not offend the referral sources or buyers? Do they add something positive to your marketing effort? Keep in mind that you are placing all your hard work of developing these clients in the hands of your partner. Will your sales agents tell you how helpful your partner was or will they respond negatively or even worse, simply send their referrals to another mortgage banker without an explanation? If you have any doubt, then you may be better off not having a partner. But if you can develop an association with someone who projects the type of image you are comfortable with, then it is time you gave it some consideration.

A more formal and consistent partnership may also be worth considering. Recognize that not everyone in the real estate offices to which you market will like you enough to do business with you. That is simply the rule of statistical probability and nothing personal. This business is simply the law of large numbers; market to enough people and if only an average percentage respond favorably to you, then you win. Sometimes those statistics can be improved by judiciously establishing a partnership with another loan officer with a somewhat different personality to create balance in your marketing effort. For example, if you are very out-going and personable, you may find it productive to develop a partnership with another person who is more low-key and analytical. If you are female, you may consider partnering with a male. Naturally, the opposite applies as well. To the sales agents who may be overwhelmed by your dynamic personality, the more reserved personality of your partner may have appeal. The key is balance and giving every referral source something to like in your partnership.

Before you commit to a full time partnership, you need to give it a lot of thought. Understand right from the beginning that no partner is ever perfect. Even if you think they are perfect, chances are they will not think you are. Recognize that you will have differences and plan for it right up front. Talk with the potential partner about it before you get into an agreement. If you both understand that you will have differences and feel you can deal with them, you should arrange to have a weekly discussion of the partnership where you can openly discuss problems. Nearly every relationship that has deteriorated, be it a business partnership, marriage or other association, had generally done so due to lack of communication. If you can discuss your problems and concerns freely and openly and accept suggestions and criticism from your partner, then you can easily handle the more mundane business aspects of a partnership.

Among the advantages of the full time partnership is the 100% availability of at least one of the partners. You will never lose business because you were not available that night or because you went to dinner with your spouse or took your children to a movie. It also means that the borrowers on loans in process will have someone to call if they have a problem or question. It means that there is someone to follow up on your loans while you are away. Of greatest importance is the synergy that can be created by two people working in tandem.

If you do enter into a partnership, you can potentially double the number of referral sources to whom you market. For example, if you normally call on thirty offices and see them once each month, now you can call on sixty offices and see them every other month. Your partner will call on the same sixty offices, seeing them in the intervening weeks between your visits. For there to be a benefit there must be more business generated than the total of what the two of you would produce individually. In some instances, generating the same amount of business that you both had individually is satisfactory because it still adds someone to give you some relief when you need a break.

Plan to visit all the offices together once every four to six months. It helps instill the partnership relationship with the real estate agents and, most importantly, it gives each of you the opportunity to introduce the partner to the agents in the office whom they have not met. It is also a good time to help the partner develop a stronger relationship with the agents with whom they have not done well, and vice-versa. Another advantage is that if you have "call reluctance" where you are hesitant to pick up the phone to call a referral source or go into an office or approach any agent, the "strength in numbers" that a partnership fosters can be of immense help.

There are of course a number of problems that a partnership can cause. First of all, you need to let everyone know that you are partners, that you work together and that you do not compete with one another. Get a professional photograph of the two of you together rather than using two individual photos and use that photo on all your marketing material. All your rate sheets and other marketing material should have both of your names and phone numbers as well as your joint photo. If you do not put pictures on nearly everything, it will take longer for the sales agents to remember that you are partners and which name goes with each face.

Among the problems you may face is the issue where one loan officer feels they are working harder than their partner and believes they are responsible for more of the business. This is a very common problem as everyone feels that they are working harder than their partner. If you can resolve the "who is working harder" dilemma, then the issue of who is responsible for the business can be easily resolved by giving credit for the loan to the person who prepares the loan application. Usually, the sales agent will call the loan officer they are most comfortable with to handle the application. If it is an on-line application, then equal credit goes to each partner. You may also decide to share every loan equally. As in everything else, this is your decision.

But maybe you already have a partner. Too often a loan officer takes for granted the most effective partner they could ever have; their loan processor. Think about it for a minute or two. Your processor will probably have more contact with your customers and referral sources than you may have. If you are willing to consider a partner, there are several reasons why you may want to consider your processor as a partner. Of course, you will have to arrange for additional compensation to cover the extra time and effort they have to invest in the partnership, but it could be the best investment you ever make.

Your processor usually knows more about your loans in process than anyone else could possibly know. Therefore, if you get a call from an agent or borrower about a loan, your processor will be able to answer the question where another loan officer will usually be unable to provide as much information. It is also very likely that any questions about qualifying buyers or the parameters of loan programs can also be answered by the processor. And, in the event it becomes necessary, the processor is generally very well qualified to prepare a loan application or handle any other task usually assumed by the loan officer.

If your processor is not willing to sacrifice some of their otherwise free time, then you need to consider whether to switch to a processor who is interested in working with you or make an arrangement with another loan officer or simply have no partner at all.

Before you approach another loan officer or a processor about being your partner, be certain to determine whether your employer permits partnership arrangements. Know in advance if they will split the payment on a loan between two people. Splitting fees after one partner has absorbed taxes and other deductions becomes more complex. When that happens, the individual receiving payment from the company usually keeps 65% of the total (less the deductions) while the partner receives 35%. In many cases when the processor becomes the partner, the loan officer simply pays them a flat fee per loan or a percentage of the total fee.

Having a partner helps keep you fresh and rested. Without that relief, you could be a candidate for burn-out. While a partner may not be right for you, at least consider the option.

Chapter 26
All the Puzzle Pieces Come Together

Bringing all the diverse pieces of the mortgage banking puzzle together in a focused business plan is what will ultimately determine the level of success that you achieve as a mortgage banker. Well, that and the time, commitment and sacrifice that you must invest in your career.

There is enormous sacrifice necessary for optimum success. This means much less time with your family and friends and fewer days off to relax. You must construct a highly effective daily plan then compress your schedule so that you accomplish much more in shorter time spans.

To fully understand what you need to do, you must have read this entire book. Absent that, these puzzle pieces will simply not fit together.

The order in which you should build your marketing plan should be thought of in terms of what you would do if you just moved to a new city where you knew no one. What would you do to become the most successful mortgage banker in that market? Based on having read the material in the preceding chapters you might consider the approach described below:

1. Determine the geographic area where you are going to work and identify the Zip Codes for that area. If you are torn between keeping your market more confined or expanding to an adjacent Zip Code, you should seriously consider the larger market option.

2. Obtain the list of professionals licensed by the state that are part of your target market.

3. Sort the list of licensed professionals to extract only those in the Zip Codes where you plan to market your services.

4. Create up to three database formats. One format is for the business units, be they real estate brokerage firms, building contractors, accounting firms or local furniture retailers. A second format is for specific individual referral sources within those businesses such as the real estate agent, lawyer, accountant and those friends and others who may serve as referral sources. And finally, a third database format, for your borrower clients. There isn't too much difference in the last two databases so it won't hurt if you simply use the same format even if some of the data fields are left empty. Keep an unused master copy of each database format that you can copy when you need it.

5. Set up a separate folder on your computer for each client group: borrowers, real estate industry, professional practitioners, retail merchants and miscellaneous referral sources. Then create a sub-folder for each company in each of those groups and then an additional sub-folder for each individual at each company, such as the agents in a real estate firm.

6. Prepare your "Introducing Your Mortgage Banker" brochure.

7. Send introductory letters to every potential referral source along with a copy of your brochure. You will probably want to send a set amount each day or week to spread the cost over a long period of time and to give you time to follow-up with those to whom you have already mailed the letters. It is easiest to start

with mailing to all your friends, letting them know that you are now in mortgage banking or that you have moved your mortgage banking practice to another firm or simply a reiteration of the fact that you are a mortgage banker. Include a mention that if they, or any of their other friends, associates or colleagues require mortgage financing, that you will be happy to assist them and that you will appreciate the referral. Of course, you should include a copy of your "Introducing Your Mortgage Banker" brochure. While your friends already know you, this is an opportunity to present the professional side of you. The next groups to which you should mail letters are real estate brokers, agents and other real estate industry related businesses. Then mail to prospective professional practice referral sources.

8. Call the managing broker of each real estate office in your Zip Code territory identified from your list of real estate licensees, Realtors® Association, Multiple Listing Service or from the Yellow Pages of the local telephone directory. Set up a time to "drop by" to introduce yourself.

9. Follow up with every real estate agent that you meet while in each real estate office, as well as every agent assigned to that office that you did not meet while you were there.

10. Join civic groups and other community organizations and then get involved in their projects and get to know their members.

11. Make phone calls to professional referral sources to arrange to drop-by to introduce yourself.

12. Drop in to meet retailers in your area starting with those whose merchandise is at the highest dollar range.

13. Meet everyone else in town to build a network of new friends, referral sources and prospective customers.
14. Follow the work schedule outlined below.

The weekly schedule that follows is intended to give you some context for how to apply your activities to generate business. Among the most salient issues is not doing too much of one thing each day. For example, if you call three real estate brokers for appointments each day, that is enough brokers to call. Then you can call three real estate agents, but those calls are slightly different and then call three professional referral sources. Each set of calls will be slightly different. Visit a few retail merchants and stop in at a few open houses. The objective is to have a list of many different things. Although some will be similar, you will have enough variety to keep you focused. If you try to call twenty real estate agents each day, you may burn out very quickly. By spreading the calls over several days, you will still make the same number of calls.

The challenge is to take all the activities that you should complete each day and compress them into the time that is available to you. To be successful you will probably need to commit sixty hours each week to your business. However, sixty hours each week may be insufficient if you choose to do more activities or you waste any time. How you structure your work week is entirely up to you, but you should consider a minimum of ten hours per day, Monday through Friday, and five hours each on Saturday and Sunday. For better results, consider a full twelve productive hours each day for five days and a minimum of five hours each day on Saturday and

Sunday for a seventy hour work week. Just keep in mind that you need to do more than put in the hours; you need to put in the work. You may even consider taking one day off each week just to recharge yourself. There is no problem with doing that, as long as you are still putting in enough hours and completing all the work that needs to be done. Just be certain that you or someone else takes all your business calls on your day off.

For maximum effectiveness you should prepare your schedule for each day's activities during the prior evening. This way, when your feet hit the floor each morning, you can be focused on the scheduled activities without losing time thinking about what you should do that day. Besides, for many people, clarity of thought is not always present first thing in the morning.

Begin the work day by reviewing all the documents for each of your loans that is scheduled to close that day. Since many mortgage companies have their closing documents prepared from a central location and transmitted to the settlement agent by email, you should be certain that you receive a copy of the email with the documents attached. This is something that very few mortgage companies do and many resist doing, but it is a crucial function of your job and far too many loan officers leave it to the closing department to get it right. Unfortunately, they do make mistakes. Sometimes the mistakes are big, and sometimes they are small, but they are still mistakes that must be corrected. The problem is that if the documents are wrong, you are the one who will bear the brunt of the borrower's rage. And yes, there will be rage, which will reverberate through the borrower and seller if this is a purchase transaction. The settlement agent will be angry and, of course, the real estate agents will be livid.

When things go wrong, you can depend on the real estate agents telling everyone how incompetent you were because the documents were all wrong. Keep in mind, "all wrong" can mean that just one small item was in error. Devise a checklist or use the one in the Exhibits and follow it meticulously through each closing package to be certain that everything is correct. You may be surprised at how often you find errors. After you finish reviewing each file, if you find errors, immediately contact your closing supervisor to have the documents corrected and forwarded to the settlement agent, with another copy to you. Call the settlement agent and inform them that the documents previously sent contain errors and that corrected documents are being sent. Give them the phone number of your closing supervisor so they can call if the documents are not promptly received. Check the revised copy when you receive it to be absolutely certain the corrections were made and that no new errors were created.

Either you or your loan processor or assistant must follow up with each borrower who has loan documents outstanding. Incomplete loan files don't close and you don't get paid. And, if the loan doesn't close on time, the real estate agent won't be sending you more business.

You should know which referral sources you are to call that day and have a list of their names and phone numbers. You should have appointments set with the referral sources you plan to visit in person with their locations mapped out with a logical, time effective itinerary. If you are attending settlements, you need to know where they are and the time they are taking place. Since most real estate settlements take about an hour, you might consider arriving about 45 minutes after the designated settlement time so that the process is largely completed by the time you arrive. This will eliminate spending a lot of time sitting through a boring document signing process and make you appear to be too busy to get there at the beginning. However, it will get you there before it ends so that you can answer any relevant questions and most importantly, meet all the parties to the transaction. In most cases, you will be one of the few loan officers the settlement agent has seen at a closing. While you should attend settlements when you can, you cannot afford to invest a lot of your time sitting through a long closing. Give priority to attending appointments with referral sources. And, do not ever be late for any appointment.

The following daily schedule includes more tasks than you can possibly complete in a day's work. However if you simply start each day with the first item and move down the list as rapidly as possible, you will accomplish much. Here is how you might structure your activities:

Sample Weekly Work Schedule

Sunday	Monday	Tuesday	Wednesday	Thursday	Friday	Saturday
Attend religious services whenever your faith meets	Check accuracy of closing documents before closing	Check accuracy of closing documents before closing	Check accuracy of closing documents before closing	Check accuracy of closing documents before closing	Check accuracy of closing documents before closing	
	Review loan files in process	Review loan files in process	Review loan files in process	Review loan files in process	Review loan files in process	
	Call applicants with outstanding items	Call applicants with outstanding items	Call applicants with outstanding items	Call applicants with outstanding items	Call applicants with outstanding items	
	Attend RE sales meeting	Attend RE sales meeting	Attend RE sales meeting	Attend RE sales meeting	Attend RE sales meeting	
Attend 6 real estate or FSBO open houses	Attend 3 real estate or FSBO open houses	Attend 3 real estate or FSBO open houses	Attend 3 real estate or FSBO open houses	Attend 3 real estate or FSBO open houses	Attend 3 real estate or FSBO open houses	Attend 6 real estate or FSBO open houses
	Call 3 professional referrals sources for appointments	Call 3 professional referrals sources for appointments	Call 3 professional referrals sources for appointments	Call 3 professional referrals sources for appointments	Call 3 professional referrals sources for appointments	
	Call 3 Real Estate managing brokers for appointments	Call 3 Real Estate managing brokers for appointments	Call 3 Real Estate managing brokers for appointments	Call 3 Real Estate managing brokers for appointments	Call 3 Real Estate managing brokers for appointments	Conduct a homebuyers seminar
	Call 3 Real Estate Sales Agents for appointments	Call 3 Real Estate Sales Agents for appointments	Call 3 Real Estate Sales Agents for appointments	Call 3 Real Estate Sales Agents for appointments	Call 3 Real Estate Sales Agents for appointments	
	Call 3 relocation companies for appointments	Call 3 relocation companies for appointments	Call 3 relocation companies for appointments	Call 3 relocation companies for appointments	Call 3 relocation companies for appointments	Make 3 RE drop in sales calls
	Call 3 corporate HR departments for appointments	Call 3 corporate HR departments for appointments	Call 3 corporate HR departments for appointments	Call 3 corporate HR departments for appointments	Call 3 corporate HR departments for appointments	
	Make 3 RE drop-in sales calls	Make 3 RE drop-in sales calls	Make 3 RE drop-in sales calls	Make 3 RE drop-in sales calls	Make 3 RE drop-in sales calls	
	Make 3 retail merchant drop-in sales calls	Make 3 retail merchant drop-in sales calls	Make 3 retail merchant drop-in sales calls	Make 3 retail merchant drop-in sales calls	Make 3 retail merchant drop-in sales calls	
	Attend appt. with professional referral sources	Attend appt. with professional referral sources	Attend appt. with professional referral sources	Attend appt. with professional referral sources	Attend appt. with professional referral sources	
	Attend appt. with RE managing brokers	Attend appt. with RE managing brokers	Attend appt. with RE managing brokers	Attend appt. with RE managing brokers	Attend appt. with RE managing brokers	

Continued on Next Page

192

Sample Weekly Work Schedule (Continued from previous page)

	Attend appt. with RE sales agents	Attend appt. with RE sales agents	Attend appt. with RE sales agents	Attend appt. with RE sales agents	Attend appt. with RE sales agents	
	Attend appt. with relocation dept.	Attend appt. with relocation dept.	Attend appt. with relocation dept	Attend appt. with relocation dept	Attend appt. with relocation dept	Attend RE settlements
	Attend appt. with corporate HR dept.	Attend appt. with corporate HR dept.	Attend appt. with corporate HR dept.	Attend appt. with corporate HR dept.	Attend appt. with corporate HR dept.	
	Attend real estate settlements	Attend real estate settlements	Attend real estate settlements	Attend real estate settlements	Attend real estate settlements	
Return phone calls from referral sources	Return phone calls from referral sources	Return phone calls from referral sources	Return phone calls from referral sources	Return phone calls from referral sources	Return phone calls from referral sources	Return phone calls from referral sources
Return phone calls from prospective borrowers	Return phone calls from prospective borrowers	Return phone calls from prospective borrowers	Return phone calls from prospective borrowers	Return phone calls from prospective borrowers	Return phone calls from prospective borrowers	Return phone calls from prospective borrowers
Handwrite note cards to each new contact	Handwrite note cards to each new contact	Handwrite note cards to each new contact	Handwrite note cards to each new contact	Handwrite note cards to each new contact	Handwrite note cards to each new contact	Handwrite note cards to each new contact
Update referral database	Update referral database	Update referral database	Update referral database	Update referral database	Update referral database	Update referral database
Prepare letters to referral sources	Prepare letters to referral sources	Prepare letters to referral sources	Prepare letters to referral sources	Prepare letters to referral sources	Prepare letters to referral sources	Prepare letters to referral sources
Mail letters & cards to referral sources & new contacts	Mail letters & cards to referral sources & new contacts	Mail letters & cards to referral sources & new contacts	Mail letters & cards to referral sources & new contacts	Mail letters & cards to referral sources & new contacts	Mail letters & cards to referral sources & new contacts	Mail letters & cards to referral sources & new contacts
	Lunch with referral source or civic club	Lunch with referral source or civic club	Lunch with referral source or civic club	Lunch with referral source or civic club	Lunch with referral source or civic club	
	Evening meeting with professional org or vol. group	Evening meeting with professional org or vol. group	Evening meeting with professional org or vol. group	Evening meeting with professional org or vol. group	Evening meeting with professional org or vol. group	
	Health Club / Gym	Health Club / Gym	Health Club / Gym	Health Club / Gym	Health Club / Gym	Health Club / Gym

This weekly schedule may look daunting, but it is more than that: it is impossible. Even if you didn't eat or sleep, you would still not complete all the tasks at the end of a 24-hour day.

So what is the purpose of a schedule so consuming that it can't be completed in a single day? The objective is to provide enough activities that completely fill your day so that you don't have a point during the day when you run out of something to do. It is assumed that you will not complete every task on the list.

193

The following "Daily Schedule" breaks out each activity and allocates the approximate amount of time it will consume, including travel time to get to or from the activities. Like the weekly schedule it is impossible to complete within a single 24-hour day.

Of course, if you closely examine the schedule you will notice that a number of activities are unlikely to occur every day. For example, you do not need to examine loan closing documents if you don't have loans closing that day. If your processor or assistant can make the follow-up calls to borrowers with outstanding documents, then you can cross that off your list. Just make absolutely certain that someone takes care of that task. You will probably not have a real estate office sales meeting every day and there may not be any open houses scheduled during most weekdays. Also, please note that while I have included the attendance of religious services on Sunday, don't be offended if your religion conducts their service on some other day. I chose Sunday simply because many religions meet on that day and for the most practical reason that the Sunday column on the chart had space available. You probably get the idea. These schedules are things that you should do each day if there is a need or an opportunity. On those days when some activities are not applicable you have an opportunity to focus on other tasks. Just don't waste time; keep moving.

When you set up your own daily work schedule, understand that what you don't complete today can be carried over until tomorrow. The key is to keep moving ahead, to complete as many tasks as you possibly can that have the potential to develop business relationships that can generate mortgage loan volume. Compress your work schedule to jam every possible activity into your work day. In other words, don't procrastinate and don't waste time. Success comes when you consistently, efficiently and effectively execute the equivalent of a full court press.

Time Application of Daily Activities

ACTIVITY	TIME AT ACTIVITY	TRAVEL TIME TO OR FROM ACTIVITY	TOTAL TIME
Drive to your office		30	30
Check accuracy of closing documents before closing (Assume two closing per day)	30		30
Review loan files in process (Assume thirty total files in processing – review 1/3 or 10 files each day)	50		50
Call applicants with outstanding items (Assume five need calls @ 5 minutes each or have your processor or assistant make the calls)	30		30
Attend real estate office sales meeting (Allow 40 minutes plus 20 minutes travel)	40	20	60
Attend 3 real estate agent or FSBO open houses - 6 on Saturday & Sunday (10 minutes for each open house)	30	40	70
Call 3 professional referrals sources for appointments (5 minutes per call)	15		15
Call 3 real estate managing brokers for appointments (5 minutes per call)	15		15
Call 3 real estate sales agents for appointments (5 minutes per call)	15		15
Call 3 relocation companies for appointments (5 minutes per call)	15		15
Call 3 corporate HR departments for appointments (5 minutes per call)	15		15
Make 3 real estate office drop-in sales calls (20 minutes each)	60	40	100
Make 3 retail merchant drop-in sales calls (20 minutes each)	60	40	100
Attend appointment with 3 professional referral sources (15 minutes each)	45	40	85
Attend appointment with 3 real estate managing brokers (30 minutes each includes meeting agents)	90	40	130
Attend appointment with 3 real estate sales agents (15 minutes each)	45	40	85
Attend appointment with 3 relocation companies (15 minutes each)	45	40	85
Attend appointment with 3 corporate HR departments (15 minutes each)	45	40	85
Attend real estate settlements (Assume 2 settlements at 30 minutes each (last 15 minutes of closing plus 15 minutes to build rapport with attendees)	60	40	90
Return phone calls from referral sources	30		30
Return phone calls from prospective borrowers	30		30
Handwrite note cards to each new contact	60		60
Update referral database	60		60
Prepare letters to referral sources	30		30
Mail letters & cards to referral sources & new contacts	15	15	30
Lunch with referral source or civic club	90	20	110
Evening meeting with professional org or vol. group	90	20	110
Health Club / Gym	45	20	65
Homebuyer Seminar	60	20	80
Religious Service	90	20	110
Drive Home		30	30
TOTAL TIME (Minutes)	1,305	445	1,850
TOTAL TIME (Hours + Minutes)	21 hrs. 45 min.	9 hrs. 5 min.	30 hrs. 50 min

Keep in mind, some of your tasks can be performed in the morning before most referral sources are in their offices and others are well suited for the evening hours. A key to your success will be separating those tasks which must be completed during the business day from those which you can perform early in the morning or late in the evening, when direct contact with referral sources is impractical. If you focus, your real work day may look more like this:

Adjusted Weekly Work Schedule

Sunday	Monday	Tuesday	Wednesday	Thursday	Friday	Saturday
Attend religious services when your faith meets 110 min.	Check accuracy of documents before closing 30 min		Check accuracy of documents before closing 30 min		Check accuracy of documents before closing 30 min	
	Review loan 1/3rd of files in process 60 min		Review loan 1/3rd of files in process 60 min		Review loan 1/3rd of files in process 60 min	
	Call applicants with outstanding items 30 min		Call applicants with outstanding items 30 min		Call applicants with outstanding items 30 min	
		Attend RE sales meeting 60 min		Attend RE sales meeting 60 min		
Attend 6 RE agent or FSBO open houses 140 min	Attend 3 RE agent or FSBO open houses 70 min	Attend 3 RE agent or FSBO open houses 70 min	Attend 3 RE agent or FSBO open houses 70 min	Attend 3 RE agent or FSBO open houses 70 min	Attend 3 RE agent or FSBO open houses 70 min	Attend 6 RE agent or FSBO open houses 140 min
	Call 3 professional referrals sources for appts. 15 min		Call 3 professional referrals sources for appts. 15 min		Call 3 professional referrals sources for appts. 15 min	
		Call 3 RE managing brokers for appts. 15 min		Call 3 RE managing brokers for appts. 15 min		Conduct a homebuyers seminar 80 min
	Call 3 RE Sales Agents for appointments 15 min		Call 3 RE Sales Agents for appointments 15 min		Call 3 RE Sales Agents for appointments 15 min	
	Call 3 corporate HR departments for appointments 15 min	Make 3 RE drop-in sales calls 100 min	Call 3 corporate HR departments for appointments 15 min	Make 3 RE drop-in sales calls 100 min	Call 3 corporate HR departments for appointments 15 min	Make 3 RE drop in sales calls 100 min
	Call 3 relocation companies for appointments 15 min		Call 3 relocation companies for appointments 15 min		Call 3 relocation companies for appointments 15 min	
	Make 3 retail merchant drop-in sales calls 85 min		Make 3 retail merchant drop-in sales calls 85 min		Make 3 retail merchant drop-in sales calls 85 min	

Continued on next page

Adjusted Weekly Work Schedule (Continued from previous page)

	Attend appt. with 3 relocation companies 85 min	Attend appt. with 3 professional referral sources 85 min	Attend appt. with 3 relocation companies 85 min	Attend appt. with 3 professional referral sources 85 min	Attend appt. with 3 relocation companies 85 min	
	Attend appt. with 3 RE managing brokers 130 min		Attend appt. with 3 RE managing brokers 130 min		Attend appt. with 3 RE managing brokers 130 min	
	Attend appt. with 3 corporate HR dept. 85 min	Attend appt. with 3 RE sales agents. 85 min	Attend appt. with 3 RE sales agents. 85 min	Attend appt. with 3 RE sales agents. 85 min	Attend appt. with 3 corporate HR dept. 85 min	
	Attend 2 RE settlements 90 min		Attend 2 RE settlements 90 min		Attend 2 RE settlements 90 min	
Return phone calls from referral sources 30 min	Return phone calls from referral sources 30 min	Return phone calls from referral sources 30 min	Return phone calls from referral sources 30 min	Return phone calls from referral sources 30 min	Return phone calls from referral sources 30 min	Return phone calls from referral sources 30 min
Return phone calls from borrowers 30 min	Return phone calls from borrowers 30 min	Return phone calls from borrowers 30 min	Return phone calls from borrowers 30 min	Return phone calls from borrowers 30 min	Return phone calls from borrowers 30 min	Return phone calls from borrowers 30 min
Handwrite note cards to each new contact 60 min	Handwrite note cards to each new contact 60 min	Handwrite note cards to each new contact 60 min	Handwrite note cards to each new contact 60 min	Handwrite note cards to each new contact 60 min	Handwrite note cards to each new contact 60 min	Handwrite note cards to each new contact 60 min
Update database 60 min	Update database 60 min	Update database 60 min	Update database 60 min	Update database 60 min	Update database 60 min	Update database 60 min
Prepare letters to referral sources 30 min		Prepare letters to referral sources 30 min		Prepare letters to referral sources 30 min		Prepare letters to referral sources 30 min
	Mail letters & cards to referral sources & new contacts 30 min		Mail letters & cards to referral sources & new contacts 30 min		Mail letters & cards to referral sources & new contacts 30 min	
		Lunch with referral source or civic club meeting 110 min		Lunch with referral source or civic club meeting 110 min		
		Evening meeting with professional org or vol. group 110 min		Evening meeting with professional org or vol. group 110 min		
		Health Club / Gym 65 min		Health Club / Gym 65 min		Health Club / Gym 65 min
460 minutes	**935 minutes**	**910 minutes**	**935 minutes**	**910 minutes**	**935 minutes**	**595 minutes**
7 hrs., 40 min.	**15 hrs., 35 min**	**15 hrs., 10 min**	**15 hrs., 35 min**	**15 hrs., 10 min**	**15 hrs., 35 min**	**9 hrs., 55 min**

Weekly total: 5,680 minutes or 94 hours and 10 minutes

Chapter 27
Conclusion

You should now know how to perform all the functions of a mortgage banker at the highest level. The only thing remaining is for you to create your business plan, commit to the essential sacrifices and to execute the tasks each and every day with proficiency and consistency. You can do it, because other people have done it; they are no different than you, except that you are probably better prepared and willing to work harder. And now, you know exactly what to do.

Ultimately, your success will be determined not just by how smart you are or how hard you work or the number of hours that you commit to building your mortgage banking practice but also by how well you integrate your referral sources into your personal life. Include them in your backyard bar-b-que or picnic, an afternoon at a sporting event, attending their company's annual holiday party (if you are invited), going as a group to concerts and plays, as well as any other event in which you or they have an interest. Through all of this you will be integrating yourself into their lives, both business and personal.

Your referral sources are your new best friends. If you fail to develop that personal connection with the real estate brokers and agents and the other referral sources in your market, your effort to generate business will be much more difficult. As you develop friendships with your business sources, the business will come to you much more easily. Of course, you still need to put in the hours and complete every task on the daily schedule, but the personal relationships that you develop along the way are what will bring the business to you.

There is no easy way to become a successful mortgage banker, but there is a way that is virtually guaranteed and that is the way described in this book. Follow the roadmap that has been provided and execute each and every task and the related detail with precision, persistence, competence and a sense of humor and your success will be assured.

Exhibits

The sample letters and personal handwritten note samples that are provided are simply to give you an idea of the type of letter or note to write. While it is possible to provide a full catalogue of letters and notes, it was intentionally not done so that loan officers would not copy them verbatim, causing the referral sources in the same marketing area to receive letters from different loan officers that are exactly the same. That would be embarrassing and negate a lot of the effort to make the relationships seem more personal.

When crafting your own letters and notes, prepare a number of standard texts and then use them as a guide when writing actual letters and notes to your borrowers and referral sources. By having a "form letter" ready to use, you can easily customize it to each situation. That "form" will save a lot of time and minor customization will make each letter and note seem personal and specific to each situation.

Take great care in preparing communication with everyone with whom you correspond. Proper grammar is essential in everything you write and neat handwriting is important for the note cards (if you want the recipient to actually be able to read what you wrote).

After each letter or note is written, be absolutely certain to proof read what you wrote. We don't always rite what we thunk we rote.

LETTER 1 Introduction from your company management announcing your appointment as a new loan officer

XYZ MORTGAGE COMPANY
1234 Main Street
Anytown, US. 99999

February 30, 2099

<RPrefix> <RFirstName> <RMNI> <RLastName>, <RSuffix)
<Number> <Street>, <Apt>
<City>, <State> <Zip>

Dear <RFirstName>,

I am very pleased to announce that JANE SMITH will now be representing XYZ MORTGAGE COMPANY in this area. With JANE'S eight years of mortgage industry experience you can expect to benefit from her exceptional knowledge and exemplary service to help you complete a greater number of sales and put more brokerage fees in your pocket.

When you refer a homebuyer to a mortgage loan officer, you are virtually placing your brokerage fee in their hands. The knowledge, competence and human relations skill displayed by your loan officer not only determines whether the loan will be approved and the sale closes, but it also determines whether you get the critical repeat business and referrals from your clients. With JANE as your mortgage partner, supporting you at each step along the way, every transaction is in the very best hands.

Although JANE will contact you personally to introduce HERSELF, you may want to talk with HER now to be certain that you and your clients are on HER priority list. You may reach JANE directly at 999-999-9999.

I have included a brochure with some information about Jane and her mortgage industry experience, as well as her extensive community involvement. When choosing a mortgage loan officer, you simply can't do better.

Naturally, if you are already working with an XYZ MORTGAGE COMPANY loan officer, please continue to work with that representative. I am certain that your XYZ MORTGAGE COMPANY experience will continue to be exemplary.

Sincerely,

JOHN Z. JONES
Executive Vice President

LETTER 2 Introductory letter from the loan officer

XYZ MORTGAGE COMPANY
1234 Main Street
Anytown, US. 99999

February 30, 2099

<RPrefix> <RFirstName> <RMNI> <RLastName>, <RSuffix)
<Number> <Street>, <Apt>
<City>, <State> <Zip>

Dear <RFirstName>,

It is my great pleasure to tell you of my new association with XYZ MORTGAGE COMPANY. I believe that you and your clients will benefit from it as well.

During the past eight years, I have served hundreds of clients by providing them with exemplary service. I have a broad range of experience in mortgage banking and related fields, which has been of enormous benefit to the real estate agents that I serve and, of course, to our mutual clients.

During the next few weeks, I hope that we will have an opportunity to sit down and talk about how we can work together to build your real estate practice. If you would like to talk with me in the interim, please call me directly at 999-999-9999.

Enclosed are several of my business cards and some valuable coupons that will save your buyers $500 on their closing costs. Please share them with your clients. You may also offer some of the coupons to your colleagues or any friends and neighbors, who may want to refinance their present mortgage.

Also included is a brochure with a little more information about my experience. I think it is important that you know about the loan officer to whom you are entrusting your clients and your commission check.

I look forward to working with you.

Sincerely,

JANE SMITH
Mortgage Banker

LETTER 3 Introductory letter to a professional referral source (Include your mortgage banker brochure and a couple business cards)

XYZ MORTGAGE COMPANY
1234 Main Street
Anytown, US. 99999

February 30, 2099

<RPrefix> <RFirstName> <RMNI> <RLastName>, <RSuffix)
<Number> <Street>, <Apt>
<City>, <State> <Zip>

Dear <RFirstName>,

In the course of your professional practice there may be an opportunity to assist your clients by referring them to a mortgage banker when they need help with financing for the purchase of a home or to refinance an existing property or even to obtain a home equity loan or line of credit.

When you refer your clients to me, they will benefit from my 99 years of lending experience and a very high level of mortgage banking services, similar to what they would receive in a financial institution's private banking department, just at much lower cost.

Should you personally require mortgage financing I am happy to assist. In addition to our extensive selection of loan programs and great rates you will benefit from a professional courtesy discount of $500 off our already low fees.

In the next few days I will call you to see when you may have a few minutes available for me to stop by your office to introduce myself. If I can be of assistance to you in the interim, please give me a call. My direct cell phone number is 999-999-9999.

I look forward to meeting you.

Sincerely,

JANE SMITH
Mortgage Banker

LETTER 4 Thank you letter from the loan officer to the real estate agent or builder after meeting with them

XYZ MORTGAGE COMPANY
1234 Main Street
Anytown, US. 99999

February 30, 2099

\<RPrefix> \<RFirstName> \<RMNI> \<RLastName>, \<RSuffix)
\<Number> \<Street>, \<Apt>
\<City>, \<State> \<Zip>

\<RNickName>,

It was a genuine pleasure meeting and talking with you on TUESDAY.

There is a great deal that we can accomplish by working together to build a strong and consistent referral business of buyers and borrowers. I am confident that we can become a highly effective business development team.

As soon as you have contact with a prospective buyer, please call me with their name and phone number so that I can get them pre-approved for financing. That will save you a great deal of time and effort by eliminating those prospects who can't qualify for financing and locking in those who are qualified.

If you need mortgage rates or loan product information, please call me or you may get the most current information at my web site: www.xyzmortgage.com/jsmith.

Let me know how I may help you. You can always reach me on my cell phone at 999-999-9999.

I look forward to working with you.

Jane

205

PERSONAL NOTE #1 (hand written)

John,

Thank you for taking time to meet with me today.

It was a genuine pleasure talking with you about how we may work together for the benefit of our mutual clients.

I have added you to my distribution list so that you will receive my current rates and program information. Of course, you can always get the most recent information at my web site: www.xyzmortgage.com/jsmith.

Please let me know when you talk with a prospective buyer and I will handle the pre-approval process and promptly get a response back to you.

Thanks,

Jane

PERSONAL NOTE #2 (printed on personal letterhead) Note to personal friends (include a postage paid return envelope and a pre-printed card with space for them to write the name and phone number of up to five prospective clients).

Bob & Sue,

As you probably know, in my mortgage banking career I depend on my friends and clients to refer new clients to me.

Please take a minute and think about who you know that I may be able to assist with financing for the purchase of a new home or the refinance of their current property. Maybe they are looking for a better rate, more appropriate loan terms or to remodel or build an addition to their home. Think of all of your friends, relatives, colleagues, acquaintances or neighbors who may benefit from the service that I offer.

I believe that your friends will be very appreciative of the personal referral because I make a concerted effort to take exceptional care of my clients with great rates and exemplary service.

Included is a card with space for you to jot down the names and phone numbers of people who you feel could benefit from my mortgage banking services. Please put the card in the enclosed envelope and drop it in the mail; I look forward to receiving it.

Many thanks for your support and for your friendship.

Jane

Sample brokerage firm database profile page

BROKERAGE FIRM PROFILE

Company Name   _____

Fictitious Name   _____

Street Address   _____

City/State/Zip   _____

Telephone   _____

Fax   _____

E-Mail Address   _____

Web Address   _____

Owner/Manager   _____

Additional Staff   _____

_____

_____

_____

_____

Affiliated Companies

Parent Company   _____

Title Company   _____

Insurance Agency   _____

Mortgage Company _____

Other   _____

Primary Lenders   _____

_____

_____

Additional Information   _____

_____

_____

_____

_____

_____

_____

_____

_____

(Continued on next page)

Sales Agents (Continued from previous page)

_____
_____
_____
_____
_____
_____
_____
_____
_____
_____
_____
_____
_____
_____
_____
_____
_____
_____
_____
_____
_____
_____
_____
_____
_____
_____
_____
_____
_____
_____
_____
_____
_____

Sample database profile page

SALES AGENT PROFILE

Name _____
Home Address _____   ┌─────────────┐
City / State / Zip _____   │   │
Cell Phone _____   │   Photo   │
Home Phone _____   │   │
Personal Fax _____   │   │
Birth Date _____   └─────────────┘

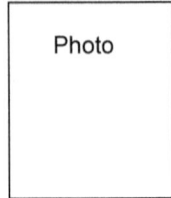

Current Preferred Lender _____
Other Lenders _____
_____
_____

Agent's Prior Business _____
    Experience _____
Education _____
Hobbies, Clubs, Etc. _____
Name of Spouse _____
Spouse's Occupation _____

Names of Children	YOB	Schools	Activities
_____	____	_____	_____
_____	____	_____	_____
_____	____	_____	_____
_____	____	_____	_____

Miscellaneous Information

_____
_____
_____
_____
_____
_____
_____
_____
_____
_____
_____
_____

210

SETTLEMENT DOCUMENT CHECKLIST

Borrower	_____	Street Address	_____
Co-Borrower	_____	City, State, Zip	_____

Appraised Value	$_____	Monthly P&I	$_____	LTV - 1st Mtg.	_____%
Purchase Price	$_____	Real Estate Taxes	$_____	LTV - 2nd Mtg.	_____%
First Mtg. Amt.	$_____	Homeowners Ins.	$_____	TLTV	_____%
Sec. Mtg. Amt.	$_____	Other _____	$_____	Interest Rate	_____%
First Mtg. Term	_____	Other _____	$_____	Origination Fee	_____%
First Mtg. Type	_____	Monthly Total	$_____	Discount Points	_____%

Item	√	Reference
Borrower's Name(s)		Confirm name with borrower(s) as to how it should appear on the documents, or how it is on current deed
Loan Approval		Confirm Loan Amount, LTV, Rate, Term and approval signatures on inside flap
Account Number		Verify Loan Account Number is correct
Interest Rate		Loan Approval / Original URLA
Per Diem		Calculate daily rate plus total through end of month
Origination Fee		Compare with Loan Approval
Discount Points		Compare with Loan Approval
Closing Instructions		Verify Amount & Totals - **Are debts that are required to be paid itemized for pay-off?**
P&I Payment		Calculate payment
Legal Description		Is the Legal Description the same on the Survey, Deed, Mortgage or Deed of Trust Tax Record, Title Policy
Survey		Confirm legal & check boundaries or encroachments
Termite Inspection		Verify no active infestation or treatment
Title Insurance		Name same as URLA, Lenders policy amount of loan, Legal description, Schedule B, Section II
Deed of Trust/Mortgage		Address same as original URLA; Legal Description; "Purchase Money" or "Refinance" **Verify Correct Form**
PUD/Condo Rider		Is the Rider Included in loan package when applicable
ARM Disclosure or Fixed/Adj. Rider		Correct payment, adjustment dates and percentages. Be certain signed copy in file; if not send to settlement
Note/Fixed Adjustable Rate Note		Verify Borrower's Name(s) with original URLA, or if refinance match previous deed/deed of trust **Verify Form**
Truth in Lending		Amount Financed, Box checked if ARM
Occupancy Affidavit		Be certain it is included in loan package
Appraisal Disclosure		Be certain it is included in loan package
Appraisal		Be certain it is included in loan package and sufficient value for loan and copy for borrower
Credit Score Disclosure		Indicates middle credit score at top and range of scores near bottom
Credit Score Notice		Be certain it is included in loan package
Notice Regarding Negative Information		Be certain it is included in loan package
Tax ID Form (W9)		Verify Name(s) and Social Security Number
Joint Credit Notice		Be certain it is included in loan package
Right to Cancel (Refinance Only)		Be certain it is included in loan package - Last cancellation date 3 business days later than transaction date
Application		Signed by Borrower
Commitment		Signed by Lender
Initial Escrow Statement		Verify calculations - Need 12 months of MI when required, plus taxes and insurance equal annual amounts
Flood Determination Certificate		Confirm flood zone is A or C; if X or Y verify flood coverage. Verify names and property address
Flood Notice		Be certain it is included in loan package
Flood Authorization Letter		Be certain it is included in loan package
Amortization Schedule (Not on ARMs)		Be certain it is included in loan package
Name Affidavit		Check names from credit report, pay stubs, W-2 Forms to be certain all variations are included
Errors & Omission		Confirm form is enclosed and complete (last page of package)
Hazard Insurance		Lower of the Appraised Value of improvements or the Loan Amount
Mortgage Insurance Disclosure		Be certain it is included in loan package
Mortgage Insurance Notice		Be certain it is included in loan package

Number of Loans Needed to Earn $1,000,000 Annually

Basis Point Compensation Plans

Average Loan Amount	Compensation Rate					
	30 bps	40 bps	50 bps	60 bps	70 bps	80 bps
$150,000	2,222	1,667	1,334	1,111	952	833
$200,000	1,667	1,250	1,000	833	714	625
$250,000	1,333	1,000	800	667	571	500
$500,000	667	500	400	333	286	250
$750,000	444	333	267	222	190	167
$1,000,000	333	250	200	167	143	125

Flat Fee Compensation Plans

	Compensation Rate					
	$500	$1,000	$1,500	$2,000	$2,500	$3,000
Number of Loans Required	2,000	1,000	667	500	400	334